COMBAT AIRCRAFT SERIES

CW00820461

Modern Soviet Fighters

MIKE SPICK

OSPREY PUBLISHING LONDON

Published in 1987 by
Osprey Publishing Ltd.
Member Company of the George Philip Group
12–14 Long Acre, London WC2E 9LP

British Library Cataloguing in Publication Data

Spick, Mike
  New MiG fighters.–(Osprey combat
  aircraft).
  1. MiG (Fighter planes)
  I. Title
  623.74'63   UG1242.F5

ISBN 0-85045-769-6

Typeset by Flair plan Photo-typesetting Ltd.
Printed by Dah Hua Printing Press Co. Ltd., Hong Kong

Designed by Little Oak Studios
Colour artworks: Mike Keep
Cutaway drawing: © Pilot Press Ltd.
Photographs: The publishers wish to thank the following
for supplying the photographs reproduced in this book:
US Department of Defense, Royal Swedish Air Force,
MARS, Tass, Klaus Niska/MARS, Michael J. Gething.

The Author

MIKE SPICK has had a lifelong interest in military
aviation, and is author of several technical books and
articles in aviation magazines covering various aspects of
the subject. One of his leisure pursuits, wargaming, led
him to a close study of air warfare, combat aircraft
development and the evolution of air combat tactics, on all
of which he has written extensively. His other books in this
series are *F-15 Eagle* and *American Spyplanes*.

Contents

1
Background

THE SPLIT between East and West arising from the so-called "Cold War" of the late 1940s and 1950s gave rise to two alliances, NATO and the Warsaw Pact, each of which regarded the other as a potential threat to world peace, and therefore as the most likely opponent in the event of hostilities. It is against this background that Soviet fighter development must be viewed. A fighter, of whatever nationality, is designed as a response to a threat, and must be considered in that context. Whether the threat is actual or merely projected is immaterial; moreover, as the limits of modern technology have expanded, fighter development time has increased, and until such time as a projected threat can be definitely seen not to be materializing, measures to counter it must be continued.

In the past, the Soviet aircraft industry has been noted for the quantity and simplicity of its products rather than for their technical excellence. In many ways, this has been the result of making a virtue out of a necessity, and has been born of two main factors. First, Soviet technology has consistently lagged behind that of the West, particularly in the vital fields of propulsion, metallurgy and electronics. Second, the Soviet Union is a vast country, with a long border, and effective air defence dictates the use of large numbers of fighters. By the same token, the Soviet Army is huge, with a tradition of close air support, and numerical strength is again essential. The result has been that the Soviet aircraft design bureaux have produced fighters that were in the main, simple, rugged, cheap, and easy to build in massive quantities. By contrast, the West, fully ex-

Below: Soviet aircraft have not always lagged the West: the MiG-19 was the first supersonic fighter to enter service, just ahead of the American F-100 Super Sabre. It was also the first to achieve a thrust-to-weight ratio better than 1.0. This is a Chinese-built F-6 derivative, in Pakistani service.

pecting that World War III would be nuclear, concentrated their efforts in the main on state-of-the-art interceptors and advanced weaponry, to defeat what they perceived as the major threat.

Oddly enough, the apparent backwardness of the Soviet aircraft industry was not necessarily to their disadvantage. Sheer numerical strength made the Soviet Air Forces a formidable adversary, while the cloak of secrecy that surrounded their development projects left the Western powers uncertain of the actual progress that was being made. This was compounded by the Russian ability to spring an occasional surprise: the performance of the MiG-15 over Korea, for example, came as a nasty shock to the West (although it should be said that this was only made possible by the import of British jet engine technology), while the MiG-19 was the first supersonic fighter to enter service and, incidentally, the first fighter in service to achieve a thrust-to-weight ratio exceeding unity at combat weight, although this achievement appears to have gone unrecognised at the time. All this seems to have caused a certain ambivalence among Western defence analysts, who on the one hand were ready to denounce Soviet fighters on the grounds of crudity and on the other postulated that the East might steal a march on the West at any moment. This attitude persists to the present day, perhaps with rather more justification than in the past. The result has been a see-saw between the USA and the USSR as each nation has sought to counter a real or a perceived threat.

Until about 1960, the trend of performance for both fighters and bombers was "faster and higher". From the Soviet viewpoint, the ultimate threat was the B-70 Valkyrie bomber, which was capable of Mach 3 at 80,000ft (24,400m) and which was sched-uled to enter service before 1970. This posed a formidable threat to the Soviet defences, and concentrated the minds of their fighter designers wonderfully.

Faulty intelligence

In July 1967 the MiG-25, codenamed Foxbat by NATO, was revealed to the world at large. At the time, the Western fighter with the highest performance was the very advanced Lockheed YF-12A, and when just three months later the new Russian machine broke two closed-circuit world speed records previously held by the American aircraft, the worst fears of the West seemed to have come true. This was aggravated by faulty intelligence. Foxbat had been misidentified as the MiG-23, and reports of massive production of this aircraft were coming from behind the Iron Curtain; moreover, when Soviet drones flying at previously unheard of heights and speeds were tracked by NATO radars they were erroneously identified as Foxbats also.

The result was predictable. The MiG-25 was assumed to be an interceptor and air superiority fighter with a performance and range that far outclassed anything that the West had to offer. By implication, the Soviet Union had stolen an enormous technological march on the West, adding quality to their already daunting numerical superiority. In fact, Foxbat had been no more than a brilliant expedient in pushing the technology available to its limits. It was a fast-climbing, ultra-high-altitude interceptor, with a short radius of action and no close combat capability

Below: The MiG-25 Foxbat was photographed for the first time at Domodedovo in July 1967. The commentator claimed a speed of Mach 3 and a ceiling of 30,000m (100,071ft).

at all. It is often held in the West that Foxbat was designed solely to counter the Valkyrie, and should have been dropped when that aircraft was cancelled, but this overlooks the fact that the Mach 2 B-58 Hustler was in service between 1960 and 1970, while the Mach 3 "Blackbird" series of reconnaissance aircraft also became operational during this period. It therefore seems reasonable that Foxbat development should have been continued to counter these two threats.

Although the MiG-23 was soon correctly identified as a medium-size, variable-sweep, counter-air fighter with a better range and more capable radar and missiles than the earlier MiG-21, the MiG-25 Foxbat remained a spectre that haunted Western planning conferences for many years—until 1976 in fact, when the West briefly got their hands on one and discovered just how mistaken they had been. But by this time they too had responded to the Foxbat threat as they had perceived it, with two very capable, very large and colossally expensive fighters, the F-14 Tomcat and the F-15 Eagle. Modifying the response was American experience in Vietnam, where lightweight, Soviet-designed fighters, the MiG-17, 19, and 21, had proved to be deadly opponents for the large and capable Phantom in close combat. The new American fighters had been designed both to defeat, not what the Foxbat was, but what it was thought to be, and also to prevail in a scenario in which they were heavily outnumbered by austere fighters.

"Hi-lo" mix

At this point, other factors entered the reckoning. The American super-fighters proved to be so expensive that the Tomcat was nearly cancelled, and ended up being forced to operate for the next 15 years with an engine that had been intended as as stop-gap, while Eagle procurement was severely curtailed. This made the numerical disparity even greater, and the USA introduced its own austere, lightweight fighter, optimised for close combat and affordable in reasonable numbers, to support the F-15 in what became known as the "hi-lo" mix. This was the F-16 Fighting Falcon. Meanwhile the USN augmented both its strike and defensive carrier capabilities by introducing the multi-role F/A-18 Hornet to replace its ageing Phantoms and Corsairs.

Above: The US Navy's answer to the Foxbat was the F-14 Tomcat, seen here during close combat trials against an F-4J Phantom. The Tomcat has an unparalleled kill capability.

Above: The single seat F-15 Eagle of the USAF was intended both to counter Foxbat and to hold its own in close combat against swarms of lightweight Soviet fighters.

Below: The expense of the super-fighters forced the USAF to develop an austere close combat aircraft, the F-16 Fighting Falcon, to supplement Eagles in a "hi-lo" mix.

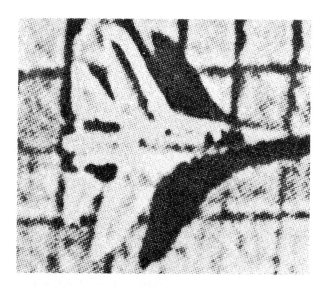

Above: Satellite photography has its limitations, as this first picture of an aircraft codenamed Ram-K shows. Thought to be an F-15 equivalent, it was identified as the Su-27.

In the air-to-air arena, this new generation of American fighters presented a new and deadly threat to the Soviet forces. Unless they could bring overwhelming numbers to bear, their fighter formations could be cut to pieces from beyond visual range and the disorganised remnants outfought in close combat. This posed a fundamental problem—whether to adhere to the traditional method of using numbers to confuse, and thus degrade, technology, or whether to develop and adopt a higher grade of technology at the expense of very large force sizes.

Satellite surveillance

During 1977, satellite surveillance began to detect unfamiliar shapes at the Ramenskoye Flight Test Centre, south-east of Moscow. Two of these appeared to be fighters, and they were codenamed Ram-K and Ram-L pending positive identification. For many years little was known about them, except that by Soviet standards their development had been unusually protracted. It has been speculated that they are in fact a Russian "hi-lo" mix, with Ram-K, the larger of the two, being an F-15 equivalent, and Ram-L having roughly the dimensions and performance of the F-16.

Ram-K has now been identified as the Sukhoi Su-27 Flanker, and Ram-L as the MiG-29 Fulcrum. Accurate data is still hard to come by. Six Fulcrums visited Finland in July 1986, but their dimensions

and weights are still a matter for conjecture, although it is now suggested that Fulcrum is nearer to the F/A-18 in size than the F-16. Apart from satellite photography, and a brief appearance on Soviet television, Flanker has not yet made its public début. Flanker and Fulcrum bear a certain likeness to each other, even though they are the products of different design bureaux, and a Soviet "hi-lo" mix cannot entirely be discounted. US sources have claimed that both aircraft have been equipped with modern multi-mode radars based on American technology acquired by covert means, and speculation is rife that the US super-fighters are outclassed by these new Soviet types. This hardly seems likely. The use of pirated radar and attack systems can give them no more than parity at best, and possibly a good deal less, while subsonic manoeuvre is fast approaching, if it has not already reached, a plateau. Advanced supersonic manoeuvre capability will depend on the attainment of supersonic cruising speed in military power, and we may be certain that this stage has not yet been attained. Finally, it has been rumoured that the Soviet Union is ahead of the West in infra-red detection capability. This may be so, or it could equally be another Foxbat-type canard. Nor does stealth technology appear to play much part in the design of either Flanker or Fulcrum. Doubtless these aircraft are good, but they are not ten feet tall. It should also be remembered that those responsible for fighter procurement have a vested interest in overstating a threat in order to obtain funds for further development.

It will be some considerable time before these two Soviet fighters reach operational units in significant

Below: Ram-L, seen here at the Ramenskoye Flight Test Centre, was later identified as the MiG-29 and codenamed Fulcrum. Lack of detail accounts for erroneous artwork.

Above: The aircraft considered most to resemble a Western type is the Su-24 Fencer, seen here in silhouette, but from this angle it does not resemble the F-111 at all.

numbers. The most important Soviet fighter in numerical terms is the MiG-23 Flogger, which will remain so until the end of the decade. In this context, it should be remembered that the Phantom was the most numerous American fighter as late as 1980, while the kindest comment on Flogger's capabilities is to say that it is not the best air superiority fighter in the world.

The Soviet Union is renowned for screwing every last ounce out of existing designs, and Foxbat is no exception. The ultra-high-speed requirement and the automated intercept have been abandoned, new engines and a new radar and attack systems have been fitted, a cockpit has been provided for a weapons systems officer, the structure is beefed up to allow some manoeuvre capability, and the aircraft has been redesignated MiG-31 Foxhound. It remains an interceptor, with no Western equivalent, but it has a far longer range, with a true look-down, shoot-down capability, and is more autonomous in operation than Foxbat ever was. Foxhound is believed to have first flown around 1974–75, and to have achieved IOC in 1982.

There is a tendency in the West to "mirror-image" Soviet aircraft, believing that what the West does first and best, the Russians will tend to copy. It is unhelpful to liken Soviet fast jets to American types too closely: while there may well be features in common, not too much significance should be read into them. The design details of Soviet aircraft have been arrived at for good, solid, Russian reasons, and they would have no need to slavishly copy a Western type. The exception that comes nearest to proving the rule is the Sukhoi Su-24 Fencer, the prototype of which is believed to have flown in 1970. The configuration appears to have been strongly influenced by that of the F-111, modified by a dash of the Mirage G. What is certain is that the operational requirements were much the same—good short-field performance, Mach 2 dash capability, extended range, and the ability to penetrate the defences at ultra-low level, at night or in adverse weather, and carry out very accurate attacks.

One of the new shapes seen at Ramenskoye in 1977 by a passing satellite was a rather odd-looking bird. It was at first codenamed Ram-J, but it has since been identified as the Sukhoi Su-25 Frogfoot. As it appears to be a close air support/battlefield air interdiction (CAS/BAI) aircraft, and possibly a counterinsurgency (COIN) type as well, comparisons with the American A-10 tankbuster are perhaps inevitable, especially as it bears a close resemblance to the Northrop A-9, which was the loser in the A-X competition. But all that comparisons in fact appear to reveal is that there is litte resemblance, either in performance or operational usage, apart from the fact that both aircraft are used in the close air support role.

A matter for speculation

Little is known for certain about these five modern Soviet fighters; even their exact sizes and weights are not known, with most reports conflicting, while often the engine type is still a matter for speculation. One would think that photogrammetric techniques would reveal the dimensions to within a couple of inches, but this is apparently not the case (or, if it is, the data has not yet been released). In consequence, the figures given in the following sections must be regarded as provisional, taken from what appear to be the best available sources and in some cases combined with a bit of horse sense. Certain previously released figures do not stand up to analysis, giving ridiculously high or low wing or thrust loadings, fuel fractions etc. So far as it is reasonable to do so, we have tried to reconcile the figures to give sensible answers, without departing too radically from the source material.

2

Mikoyan MiG-29 Fulcrum

UNTIL RECENTLY all that was known about the MiG-29 was of a highly speculative nature—satellite photographs that were small and lacked detail, with data and artist's impressions released by the US DoD, both of which tended to be conflicting. It was at first thought to be a Soviet counterpart of the F-16, but later it was likened to the F-18. Then, in July 1986, six Fulcrums visited the Finnish air base at Kuopio-Rissala, and the West got its first good look at this new Soviet fighter. And what an odd-looking bird it proved to be! If anything, the visit only served to increase the speculation rather than resolve it.

Two widely spaced engine nacelles set very low to the ground were surmounted by a wing of moderate sweep, with large leading-edge root extensions (LERXes) reminiscent in planform of those of the VF-17 Cobra. No attempt had been made to set the engines closer together and curve the intakes in towards them, with the result that a deep tunnel, rather like that on the F-14, was formed, although it was much narrower. The forward fuselage took the form of a nacelle set above the wing level, tapering

sharply from behind the cockpit to form a "pancake" rear fuselage ending in a boat-tail, again similar to that on the F-14. The nose seemed big enough to enclose quite a large radar antenna, and just ahead of the windshield, offset to starboard, was a transparent dome that seemed to be a housing for an infrared detection and tracking seeker. Widely spaced twin fins with a compound-sweep leading edge and cropped tips were mounted on vestigial booms outside the line of the engines, as featured on the F-15, the booms also carrying the all-moving horizontal tail surfaces. The abiding impression was of an amalgam of features taken from American fighters combined with typical MiG-bureau fins.

At the time of the visit the Finnish Air Force released some data on dimensions and weights which seemed to indicate that Fulcrum was smaller and lighter than had previously been thought, although it was still nearer to the Hornet than the Fighting Falcon in size. This data appears to be

Below: A DoD artist's impression of Fulcrum, released before the aircraft had been seen in the West. The accuracy of this illustration should be judged against that on page 11.

approximate only, and should be treated with reserve until such times as it can be confirmed or denied. The source is uncertain: if it was released to the Finns by the visiting Russian unit the possibility exists that it contains a certain amount of disinformation designed to make the wing loading look lower and the thrust loading appear higher than is in fact the case. It is noticeable that all Western analysts, attempting to scale from the available photographs, have come up with larger figures, but without using advanced photogrammetric techniques, and without an absolutely accurate reference point, this method has plenty of room for error, as an examination of the various published figures shows. This notwithstanding, it seems preferable to take the Finnish figures on trust for the time being.

Low bypass ratio turbofans

One point on which most sources seem to agree is that Fulcrum is powered by two Tumanskii R-33D turbofans, rated at 18,300lb (81.3kN) static thrust at maximum power and 11,243lb (50kN) in military power. This, if the figures obtained from Finland are correct, gives Fulcrum a thrust-to-weight ratio barely less than that of the F-15A, and rather better than that of the F-16A. The R-33D is in much the same class as General Electric's F404, and is expected to have a low bypass ratio similar to that of the American "leaky turbojet". It is also, despite reports to the contrary, the first turbofan to power an in-service Soviet fighter.

Above: Four of the six Fulcrums that visited Kuopio-Rissala in Finland in July 1986 performing a formation flypast. The unusual tail-down flight attitude can clearly be seen.

Both the layout and the configuration of the engine nacelles have aroused considerable comment. The wide spacing has been seen in some quarters as an attempt to minimise battle damage effects by locating the engines so far apart that a single hit stands little chance of knocking out both. There is also the argument that a hit on the main fuel tanks in the rear fuselage would stand less chance of spilling fuel directly into the face of the engine and starting an uncontrollable fire. On the other hand, the spacing is too wide for the first reason to be acceptable, while it also increases the vulnerability of the main tanks to a hit from the underside. The tunnel between the nacelles is rather too narrow to carry stores without considerable interference drag, and unless it is intended to carry some sort of conformal fuel tank in this position, it represents just so much wasted space.

One further reason must be considered. Turbofan development has been notoriously difficult in the West, and it is possible that Soviet engine designers are also having problems. The "straight-through" line from intake to nozzle echoes that adopted for the Tomcat, to minimise disturbance in the duct when using an engine known to be sensitive to disturbed airflow. It is therefore tempting to speculate that the Mikoyan bureau has adopted the same solution to a similar problem. Quite apart from the wasted ventral area, the tunnel between the nacelles causes extra wetted area and, with it, drag, although at the same time it does provide extra keel area for improved lateral stability. In this connection it should be noted that ventral fins, for so long a feature of Soviet fighters, are absent from Fulcrum.

Unusual intakes

The most radical feature of Fulcrum to be revealed in Finland was the intake. Two-dimensional and sharply raked, it is situated beneath the LERX to minimise flow distortion at high angles of attack (AOA), with variable multi-shock ramps to allow flight at speeds beyond Mach 2. The unusual feature is that the intakes can be sealed off when the aircraft is on the ground, air for the engine being drawn through auxiliary intakes on the top surfaces of the LERX consisting of five rectangular apertures with venetian blind-type shutters. It is not clear at present whether the main intakes are closed by movement of the compression ramps, or whether a purpose-designed surface is used. Whichever it is, a row of rectangular holes is featured along the bottom edge, the purpose of which is presumably to admit enough air to help smooth out the flow in the intake duct after it has been drawn in through the auxiliary intakes and turned through 90 degrees towards the engine face.

This unique feature appears to be an anti-FOD (foreign object damage) measure, intended to prevent the ingress of deleterious material that could damage the engine. The exact mode of operation is not known. Fulcrum can certainly taxi with the main intakes closed, and the system makes little sense unless it can accelerate to rotation speed with them closed, even if this must be done in military rather than maximum power. Accounts vary as to whether this is possible. It has also been suggested that they can be closed in flight as a "stealth" measure, but as the auxiliary intakes are located in a low-pressure area this seems highly unlikely. The rest of the design shows little evidence of stealth measures. What does seem probable is some form of automatic actuation, perhaps on take-off when the weight comes off the nose gear or a certain AOA is reached, and on landing when weight comes on the main gear or the throttles are retarded. Whatever the reason for its adoption, it seems rather a drastic measure. Operationally it would ease the problems of using a rough landing site, or a damaged airfield, and it would certainly improve the chances of a safe landing on a damaged, FOD-strewn airfield by a fuel-starved fighter. It has also been suggested that it would ease operations from a snow or slush-covered runway. These are all worthy considerations, but it is

Below: The odd inlet doors are seen in the closed position as this Fulcrum taxis in. The unusual extensions to the fin leading edge and the thick LERXes are also evident.

unlike the Soviets to be so fancy in their solutions to a well-known problem. It is arguable that the main problem arose from the basic design. The base ground clearance of the intakes is less than that of any known fast jet, even the F-16, the chin intake of which was predicted (erroneously) to be a FOD trap. The sharply raked, two-dimensional intakes are therefore ideally placed to hoover up any loose matter in their path. Given Fulcrum's unusually long gestation period before entering production, it is just possible that the magnitude of the ingestion problem was not fully appreciated until flight trials had commenced, forcing this ingenious (and rather un-Russian) solution to be developed from scratch.

Rough-site landing gear

Fulcrum's landing gear appears to bear out the assumption that the aircraft is intended for rough-site operations. Short and chunky, with oversized, low-pressure tyres, the main gear is located near the wing roots, and it retracts forwards, with the wheels turning through 90 degrees, to stow in the undersides of the LERXes. A more obvious location would have been in the sides of the engine nacelles, but apparently there is insufficient room. This is partly the cause of the lack of ground clearance beneath the lower lip of the intake: presumably in the interests of strength the gear was kept short, and this,

combined with the underwing location, has brought the nacelles very close to the ground. The main gear wells have two doors, the inners being much deeper than the outers. A landing light is mounted on each of the inner gear doors. The nose gear is a twin-wheel arrangement located under the forward fuselage, just aft of the cockpit. Surprisingly, this retracts back into the tunnel between the engine nacelles, which is another reason for assuming that no stores can be carried in this area. All wheels are painted apple green, the colour used on gun carriages of Russian armies of Napoleonic times.

It has been suggested that part of the FOD problem arises from debris kicked up by the nosewheel, but if this were the case the gear would sport a mudguard, as do so many other Soviet fighters. The shortness of the gear is such that the ground clearance of the engine nacelles is too small for weapons to be carried beneath them; the clearance is in fact so small that over-rotation on take-off or landing could easily ground the rear end, but, rather surprisingly, no protective bumper is fitted.

Almost nothing is as expected on Fulcrum, and the tailpipes are no exception. These appear to be of a curious double arrangement, each with a movable sheath surrounding a convergent/divergent

Below: Fulcrum's main gear retracts forwards to stow beneath the LERXes, but the stalky nose gear leg retracts aft. The open doors of the auxiliary inlets are visible from this angle.

("con-di") nozzle. It may be that cooling bypass air is led not only around the engine but also around the augmentor. The design might also serve to reduce the attraction of the exhaust plume to heat-seeking missiles, although this is pure speculation. It has been commented that Fulcrum is a very quiet aircraft: this is, of course, a subjective judgement, to be treated with suspicion, but it is always possible that noise reduction is a spin-off from the double nozzle.

The wings appear to have a very thin section, with a correspondingly low thickness/chord ratio. Leading-edge sweep is about 40 degrees, while the trailing edge is straight and only slightly swept. About 2 degrees of anhedral is evident, and the tips are slightly rounded. Almost the entire leading edge is occupied by what appears to be a single-piece slat or flap, which can be used to increase manoeuvre capability as well as to reduce take-off and landing speeds. The trailing edges comprise single-slotted flaps inboard and rather small, traditional ailerons outboard. There are no signs of spoilers, so presumably roll control at high speeds is augmented by differentially moving tailerons. The visitors to Finland showed no evidence of underwing hardpoints, but it is believed that there are three per side, one of which is plumbed for the carriage of drop tanks.

Ahead of the wings are large LERX, which extend to a point ahead of the windshield and which must obstruct the pilot's view downwards. Unlike those featured on American fighters, they are very deep, with a rounded leading edge which only becomes sharp where it meets the forebody. They serve multiple purposes: apart from angling the airflow into the intakes at high AOAs they generate vortices along the upper wing surfaces which inhibit spanwise flow and improve lift and high AOA handling, while at transonic and supersonic speeds they provide a destabilising effect which serves to reduce the trim drag needed to counter the effect of the centre of lift moving aft. The extra depth provided gives space for the main gear stowage, room for the auxiliary inlet shutters and probably volume for extra fuel capacity. A degree of wing/body blending is apparent on the upper surface. This is a drag-reducing feature, and is also the only visible concession to "stealth".

Internal gun

A gun is mounted close inboard in the port LERX. This has been variously described as a six-barrel Gatling type, a twin-barrel GSh-23, or a large calibre, possibly 30mm, single-barrel revolver cannon. As

Below: The engine intakes are shielded by the LERXes for high-AOA flight. Also seen here is the unusual double nozzle arrangement, the precise purpose of which is unclear.

nothing is visible apart from a stainless steel blast deflector and six small square holes, presumably for ventilation and/or cooling, situated just ahead of the auxiliary intake slots and over where the gun mechanism can be assumed to be, this is sheer guesswork, although a 23mm single-barrel weapon seems the most likely. Outboard of the gun muzzle on the leading edge are two small dielectric panels which are repeated on the starboard side; coupled with the flush aerials on the wing tips, this seems to indicate the presence of a full ECM suite, both active and passive. The air-to-air weapons fit is reported to be a mix of two or four R.23 (AA-7) Apex and two or four R.60 (AA-8) Aphid missiles, although it is thought that these will shortly be replaced by the new AA-10 medium range and AA-11 dogfight missiles.

The fuselage consists of a high-set forward nacelle containing the radar and the cockpit, which tapers sharply back from behind the canopy to form a flat pancake in the manner of the F-14. This, combined with the underslung engines, gives a deep fuselage and a correspondingly large presented area from side-on, which will make it difficult to cause an opponent to lose sight at long range by "knife-edging", rolling from a planform aspect to elevational view.

The radome is ogival, with a simple probe on the

Above: The tunnel between the engine nacelles appears to be too narrow for effective stores carriage. The tail surfaces are carried on booms like those on the F-15.

tip. It appears large enough to house an antenna of similar size to that of the APG-65 carried by the Hornet. The radar is stated to be a multi-mode, pulse-doppler type, with a look-down, shoot-down capability, based on technology covertly acquired from the United States.

Below: In the same weight and wing loading categories as the F-16C and F/A-18A, Fulcrum has a distinct advantage in thrust loading, which may give it an edge in close combat.

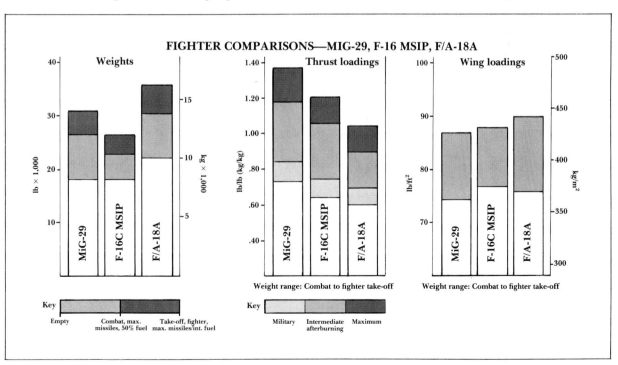

FIGHTER COMPARISONS—MIG-29, F-16 MSIP, F/A-18A

Weights

Thrust loadings

Weight range: Combat to fighter take-off

Wing loadings

Weight range: Combat to fighter take-off

Key — Empty | Combat, max. missiles, 50% fuel | Take-off, fighter, max. missiles/int. fuel

Key — Military | Intermediate afterburning | Maximum

MIKOYAN MiG-29 FULCRUM-A SPECIFICATION DATA

Dimensions
Length:	50ft 10.3in (15.50m)
Span:	34ft 5.4in (10.50m)
Height:	17ft 2.8in (5.25m)
Wing area:	358ft (33.30sq m)
Aspect ratio:	3.32

Weights
Empty:	18,000lb (8,165kg)
Fighter take-off:	31,000lb (14,061kg)
Maximum take-off:	36,000lb (16,330kg)
Combat, 50% fuel:	26,625lb (12,077kg)

Powerplant
Two Tumanskii R-33D augmented turbofans, each rated at 18,300lb (8,167kg) maximum thrust or 11,243lb (5,100kg) military thrust.

Fuel
Internal:	8,750lb (3,969kg)
External:	2,000lb (907kg)
Fraction:	0.28

Loadings
Wing, fighter, take-off:	87lb/sq ft (422kg/sq m)
Wing, combat:	74lb/sq ft (363kg/sq m)
Thrust, maximum, fighter, take-off/combat:	1.18/1.37
Thrust, military, fighter, take-off/combat:	0.73/0.84

Performance
Vmax, hi:	Mach 2.3
Vmax, lo:	Mach 1.2
Ceiling:	55,000ft (16,750m)
Initial climb rate:	50,000ft/min (254m/sec)
Take-off run:	1,640ft (500m)
Landing run:	1,475ft (450m)
Combat radius:	620nm (1,150km)
Intercept radius:	200nm (370km)

Prior to the visit to Finland, it had been assumed that the cockpit canopy would be a high-set bubble, giving the pilot an excellent all-round field of vision. In fact, it is a strange humped affair, with a wrap-around windshield raking steeply forwards and downwards, and a heavy canopy bow. Visibility is better than in previous Soviet fighters, but hardly perfect. The canopy is hinged to open at the rear (and can be left slightly open prior to take-off, which suggests a lack of air conditioning) and the rearward slope continues into the fuselage in a straight line. It is believed that a two-seat variant of the MiG-29 is under development, but it is hard to see how a second crew position can be accommodated without causing a huge and draggy hump.

The pilot is set deep in the fuselage, with the cills at shoulder level, further reducing the view out. Cockpit details are not available, but what appears to be a wide-angle head-up display (HUD) is visible in some photographs, together with other equipment which tends to obscure the forward view.

Just ahead of the windshield and offset to the right is what appears to be an infra-red seeker/tracker, housed in a transparent dome. IR detection is far from new: it has been tried extensively in the West (the last occasion was on the F-14) and found wanting, for a variety of reasons. Its appear-

Below: The MiG-29's lack of ground clearance appears to restrict the carriage of stores to underwing hardpoints, and would also seem to make engine changes rather difficult.

ance on Fulcrum can be interpreted in one of three ways. First, it has been widely touted that the Soviet Union is ahead of the West in this field; second, it is a passive target acquisition device for close combat; and third, with the B-1B already in service, combining "stealth" features and a massive defensive avionics suite, with the F-19 "stealth" fighter rumoured to be in service, and with the "stealth" oriented Advanced Technology Bomber (ATB) well into the development stage, it may well have been felt that some form of IR detection, despite its shortcomings, was better than relying totally on a radar system which just might not work. The writer is inclined to the third explanation.

To the left of the IR sensor is the aerial system of Odds Rods IFF. Two blade antennae, probably UHF radio, project beneath the cockpit, while a few feet behind it on the dorsal surface is a VHF aerial. The usual array of temperature and dynamic pressure sensors project around the cockpit. A two-piece airbrake is located in the pancake between the engines, and a braking parachute housing is in the centre of the boat-tail.

Fuel tanks must occupy much of the rear fuselage as, apart from the wings, which are certainly "wet", there is nowhere else to put them, with the possible exception of the fins. As the aft fuselage slopes sharply away behind the cockpit, with a progressive decrease in usable depth, some com-

mentators have speculated that the fuel fraction must be low and hence the aircraft must lack endurance. Appearances can be deceptive, as the F-16 proves: limited-endurance fighters went out of fashion in the Soviet Union many years ago, and it is hardly likely that Fulcrum has been designed to have a radius of action very much shorter than that of Flogger, which it is to replace.

All-moving tail surfaces

The horizontal tail surfaces are all-moving, and have the tips cropped to avoid flutter problems. They appear to be set slightly below the line of the wing, and the trailing edge extends well back past the nozzles. They may move differentially to assist roll control, but this has not been confirmed, and neither has the report that they may be of composite construction.

The tall twin fins are set well outboard, with a slight cant. The single rudders are set just below central, and the trailing edge is cranked backwards under them, while the cropped tips both have dielectric housings. The port fin carries an aerial of the type associated with the Sirena II radar warning receiver (RWR) on the trailing edge, while both trailing edges carry aerials and static dischargers.

Below: Over-rotation would risk grounding the rear end, yet no bumpers are fitted. Here, both the main intake doors and the auxiliary inlets appear to be open for take-off.

An unusual feature is that the leading edges have extensions that carry forward over the upper surface of the wing to a point close to the leading edge, where they stop quite abruptly. These extensions have been interpreted as wing fences to arrest spanwise flow, but this seems improbable as they are too far inboard. It is uncertain whether Fulcrum has a fly-by-wire control system or is conventionally stable; recent reports state the latter, but relaxed stability and FBW should not be discounted.

Superior performance

Although first seen at Ramenskoye in 1977, it was not until 1982 that Fulcrum was known to be in production, achieving initial operational capability (IOC) in 1985. When demonstrated in Finland, it was seen to have a far superior performance to that of the MiG-21bis, while the formation-keeping of the visiting unit was better than that of previous units flying Fishbeds and Floggers. As the lowest ranking Soviet pilot was a major, it can be inferred that the visitors were out to make a good impression and that all the pilots had a high experience level.

A final mystery surrounds Fulcrum. It is highly unusual for a new, state-of-the-art Soviet fighter to be demonstrated before Western observers at such an early stage in its operational career. It is equally

Above: A braking parachute is deployed on landing, and this is housed in the pancake between the engines. There is no sign of spoilers, and the outboard wing control surface appears to be a conventional aileron, while the inboard surface is a simple flap, seen deployed here.

unusual for it to be exported so soon, yet Fulcrum is expected to enter service with Syria in late 1986, and India in mid-1987. It is also known that the Indian aircraft are to be "full up" versions, and not degraded in any way by using elderly avionics. This seems strange by any standards. Is the Soviet Union prepared to risk the West knowing exactly what progress it has made by exporting these fighters, or could Fulcrum have been developed primarily for the export market to friendly or non-aligned countries? Yet another riddle remains to be answered.

It is reasonable to suppose that Fulcrum is a good, if not an outstanding, fighter. It certainly appears to have been optimised for the air-to-air role, and its rather odd configuraton would handicap it for the ground attack mission, so much valuable carrying space having been wasted. How good it is, and precisely what it is, remains to be seen. It may be a little better than the F-16 in close combat: the thrust-to-weight figures certainly suggest that it is, while the wing loading is reasonably light. While it represents a leap forward in Soviet fighter capability, it can hardly be more than a small step forward for fighter capability *per se*, if at all.

3
Sukhoi Su-27 Flanker

FIRST SPOTTED by satellite surveillance at Ramenskoye in 1977, and allocated the reporting name Ram-K, the Su-27 Flanker is even more mysterious than Fulcrum. Apart from satellite pictures, the only glimpse of it in the West to date came in December 1985, when what is believed to be an early prototype, seen flying in the late 1970s, was featured in a Soviet television programme. As is usual with new Soviet fighters, little information is available, and most of that is of a highly speculative nature. It is the old story: those who know aren't telling, while those who don't know are speculating. All that is certain about Flanker is that it is large, has various features in common with Fulcrum, and has had a protracted and troublesome development period during which major design changes had to be made.

Dimensionally it is rather larger than the American F-15 Eagle, and it weighs considerably more, although less than the F-14 Tomcat. It is widely supposed to be an F-15 equivalent (although such analogies are of dubious value), and its general similarity of appearance to Fulcrum gave rise to the Su-27/MiG-29 "hi-lo" mix theory. While credible, this is far from certain, and the likeness probably stems from the influence of TsKB, the Central Design Bureau, the function of which is to produce feasibility studies before instructing the OKBs, or design bureaux, to proceed with a project. In this case, the specifications may have included certain solutions to aerodynamic or propulsion problems, or even operational requirements. The basic similarities are the widely spaced, underslung engines, the high-set front fuselage nacelle, the twin fins, the wing planform, and the LERXes. In fact, examination reveals considerable differences between the two, which represent the individual solutions of the respective OKBs.

Below: The only photographs currently available of the Su-27 Flanker are taken from a Soviet television programme shown in December 1985, and are believed to depict a prototype flying in the late 1970s. Detail is naturally lacking, as is information about how production aircraft might differ.

SUKHOI Su-27 FLANKER-A SPECIFICATION DATA

Dimensions		Powerplant		Performance	
Length:	67ft 3.6in (21.50m)	Two Tumanskii R-29 derivatives (?) each		Vmax hi:	Mach 2.3
Span:	47ft 6in (14.50m)	rated at 28,100lb (12,750kg) maximum		Vmax lo:	Mach 1.1
Height:	18ft 0.5in (5.50m)	thrust or 15,700lb (7,123kg) military		Ceiling:	60,000ft (18,300m)
Wing area:	689sq ft (64.00sq m)	thrust.		Initial climb rate:	60,000ft/min
Aspect ratio:	3.27				(305m/sec)
		Fuel		Take-off run:	N/A
Weights		Internal:	14,330lb (6,500kg)	Landing run:	N/A
Empty:	33,070lb (15,000kg)	External:	6,864lb (3,310kg)	Combat radius:	810nm (1,500km)
Clean take-off:	49,600lb (22,500kg)	Fraction:	0.29	Interception radius:	260nm (485km)
Maximum take-off:	63,800lb (29,000kg)				
Combat, 50% fuel:	43,435lb (19,250kg)	**Loadings**			
		Wing, fighter,			
		take-off:	72lb/sq ft (352kg/sq m)		
		Wing, combat:	62lb/sq ft (301kg/sq m)		
		Thrust, maximum, fighter,			
		take-off/combat:	1.13/1.32		
		Thrust, military, fighter,			
		take-off/combat:	0.63/0.74		

The first satellite photograph released of Flanker suggested that it had variable sweep. Two possibilities exist. Either the aircraft seen was an experimental type, bearing no relationship to Flanker, or a variable-geometry (VG) prototype was actually built, and flown in comparative trials. Either way, it seems to have sunk without trace. It is, however, an interesting point that the wing planform first adopted was very similar to that considered for a fixed-wing version of Tomcat and abandoned in favour of variable sweep. Given the wide engine spacing and forward fuselage nacelle of both aircraft, the plan views were very alike.

Tremendous leap

The wide engine spacing was almost certainly adopted on recommendations from TsKB for the same reasons as that of Fulcrum, which, as we have seen, are speculative. The type of engine is not known, although the intake size seems to indicate a large turbofan, as do the released performance figures. It may be a derivative of the Tumanskii R-31, or possibly the R-29 turbojet, which may well have been used in the early prototype and development aircraft. All things considered, it is most likely to be a low bypass ratio turbofan derived from the R-29, with thrust ratings rather lower than the 30,000lb (133kN) maximum and 20,000lb (89kN) frequently ascribed to it, as a turbofan of this output, and of roughly the same size as the F100, would imply a tremendous leap in Soviet propulsion technology, and this must be doubtful.

Like Fulcrum, the intakes are two-dimensional

and sharply raked, and located beneath the LERXes. They do not, however, appear to feature (or even need) the exotic intake closing system of that aircraft, nor the equally exotic auxiliary intakes through the top surface of the LERXes. Unlike the Mikoyan fighter, the Su-27 has a lengthy undercrriage which give adequate ground clearance—which poses the question, if it could be done for one, why not the other? Multi-shock internal ramps give a Mach 2 plus capability, and the straight-through nacelles appear to bulge ventrally towards the rear, ending in an apparently conventional "con-di" nozzle, without the double sheathing of Fulcrum.

Wide engine spacing

Again like Fulcrum, the single-wheel main gear appears to be located in the wing root, and the gear retracts upwards and forwards, turning through 90 degrees for stowing. The main gear doors are in two pieces, one folding laterally down outboard, while the other folds forward, into the airflow. It is believed that the front main gear door doubles as an airbrake. The wide engine spacing and underwing gear location gives quite a wide track for stability on the ground. The nose gear is totally different from that of Fulcrum. It is much longer, and is located forward of the cockpit, rotating aft to stow beneath the cockpit. Landing light positions have not been identified, but they are probably on the nose gear leg. The nose gear appears to have a twin wheel, and this has a box-type mudguard, in common with many other Soviet fighters.

The wings are of thin section, with a 40-degree

leading-edge sweep and gently curved tips featured on the early development aircraft, together with a curving LERX reaching from 30 per cent span to a point level with the front of the cockpit. Some previously released figures suggested that the aspect ratio was high, at nearly 4, but the latest information reduces it to a more believable 3.27, slightly lower than Fulcrum but higher than the F-15. The stills from the TV programme appear to show Flanker landing, but no deployment of either leading- or trailing-edge flaps is visible. The existence of leading-edge flaps or slats is probable, but the absence of trailing-edge flaps is incredible, and the only possible inference is that the Russians did not want to give too much away.

Revised wings and LERXes

The wings and LERXes on the production aircraft have since been considerably revised. The curved tips have been straightened, and it has been stated that this is to accommodate missile launch rails. It does, however, seem far more likely that tip pods containing ECM and/or continuous-wave (CW) missile guidance gear have been substituted. The standard Soviet Sirena RWR, with 360-degree coverage, uses wing-tip aerials, and it is hard to suppose that this has been abandoned. A pod after the style of that fitted to Foxbat-E is far more probable. The LERXes, which are thinner than those of Fulcrum and more sharply edged, have also been revised, to give a straight leading edge. It can be expected that slats or flaps, optimised for manoeuvring flight, will be found on the leading edge, while the trailing edge will have single slotted flaps inboard and ailerons outboard for control in the rolling plane, supplemented by differentially moving tailerons at supersonic speeds. It is also believed that Flanker employs

Below: Flanker has various features in common with Fulcrum, such as the podded, underslung engines, the LERXes and the twin fins. It is believed to be slightly larger than the F-15, and has undergone considerable modifications since this picture was taken.

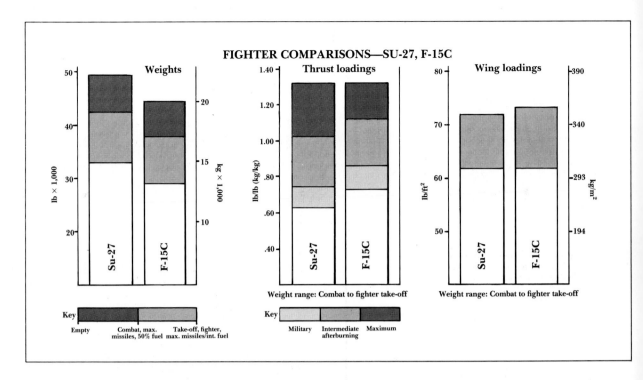

FIGHTER COMPARISONS—SU-27, F-15C

Weights

Thrust loadings

Wing loadings

Weight range: Combat to fighter take-off

Weight range: Combat to fighter take-off

Key
Empty | Combat, max. missiles, 50% fuel | Take-off, fighter, max. missiles/int. fuel

Key
Military | Intermediate afterburning | Maximum

relaxed static stability and fly-by-wire, but whether mechanical back-up is present is not clear. What is known is that the Soviet Union does have this capability, and on a fighter of this size and complexity it seems most probable that it would be used.

Large radar antenna

Like Fulcrum, the forward fuselage nacelle is set high, above the wing level. It is comparatively large, and the width is seemingly sized by the radome rather than the cross-section of the cockpit. This implies a radar antenna rather larger than that carried by the bigger Western fighters. The radar itself is supposed to be based on the AWG-9 as used on the Tomcat and acquired via Iran, with features of the Hornet's APG-65 added. It can therefore be said with some confidence that it is a multi-mode pulse-doppler type with excellent performance in long-range search and track-while-scan and probably good angular resolution, able to pick single targets out of a closely bunched formation at something more than 40nm (74km). The IR sensor dome of the Fulcrum is not repeated, but small excrescences are visible on the outer corners of the intakes. It is possible that one of these is an IR sensor, while the other may be some form of televisual aid, possibly along the lines of low-light TV (LLTV), included

Above: Flanker is larger and heavier than the F-15C, with a similar wing loading, while possessing a marginal edge in thrust loading. It should however be remembered that natural growth has made the F-15C much heavier than the F-15A, and the same may well happen to Flanker over the years.

to give positive visual identification at ranges beyond the limits of the human eye.

The canopy appears similar to that of Fulcrum, with a one piece wrap-around windshield and a rearward-hinged opening section, although the rearward taper is not so steep, owing to the greater length of the fuselage, and the general appearance is not so humped.

Beaver tail

Early prototypes are shown with a beaver tail to the pancake, although this appears to have been considerably modified on the production aircraft, which is depicted as having a central protrusion projecting back to well aft of the nozzles. This may house a braking parachute, or it might otherwise contain RWR and ECM aerials, and possibly a chaff and flare dispenser. The photographic evidence available has insufficient detail for dielectric panels and sensor pitots to be made out, and these must remain a matter for conjecture at present.

The one-piece, all-moving horizontal tail surfaces are set rather lower than the wing, and in early

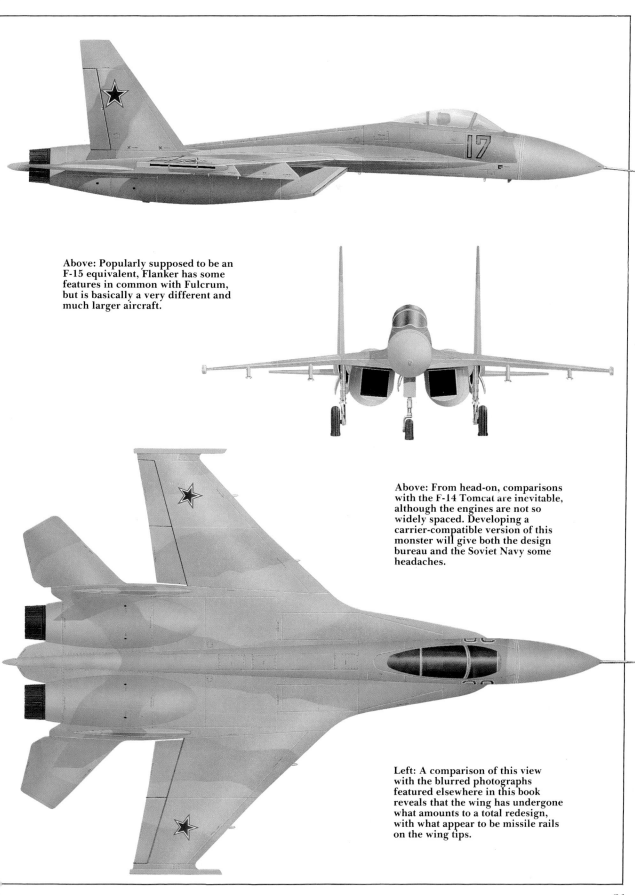

Above: Popularly supposed to be an F-15 equivalent, Flanker has some features in common with Fulcrum, but is basically a very different and much larger aircraft.

Above: From head-on, comparisons with the F-14 Tomcat are inevitable, although the engines are not so widely spaced. Developing a carrier-compatible version of this monster will give both the design bureau and the Soviet Navy some headaches.

Left: A comparison of this view with the blurred photographs featured elsewhere in this book reveals that the wing has undergone what amounts to a total redesign, with what appear to be missile rails on the wing tips.

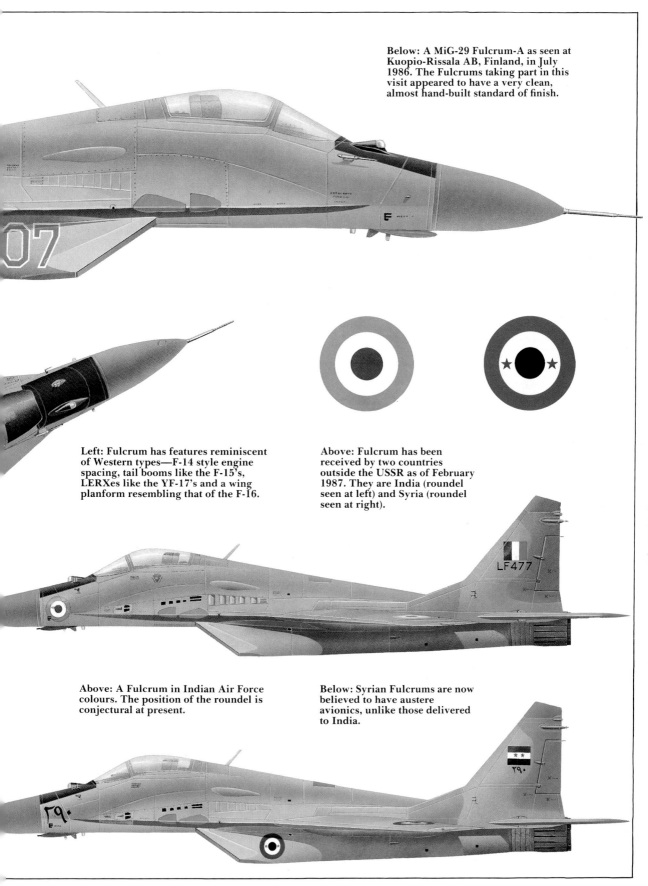

Below: A MiG-29 Fulcrum-A as seen at Kuopio-Rissala AB, Finland, in July 1986. The Fulcrums taking part in this visit appeared to have a very clean, almost hand-built standard of finish.

Left: Fulcrum has features reminiscent of Western types—F-14 style engine spacing, tail booms like the F-15's, LERXes like the YF-17's and a wing planform resembling that of the F-16.

Above: Fulcrum has been received by two countries outside the USSR as of February 1987. They are India (roundel seen at left) and Syria (roundel seen at right).

Above: A Fulcrum in Indian Air Force colours. The position of the roundel is conjectural at present.

Below: Syrian Fulcrums are now believed to have austere avionics, unlike those delivered to India.

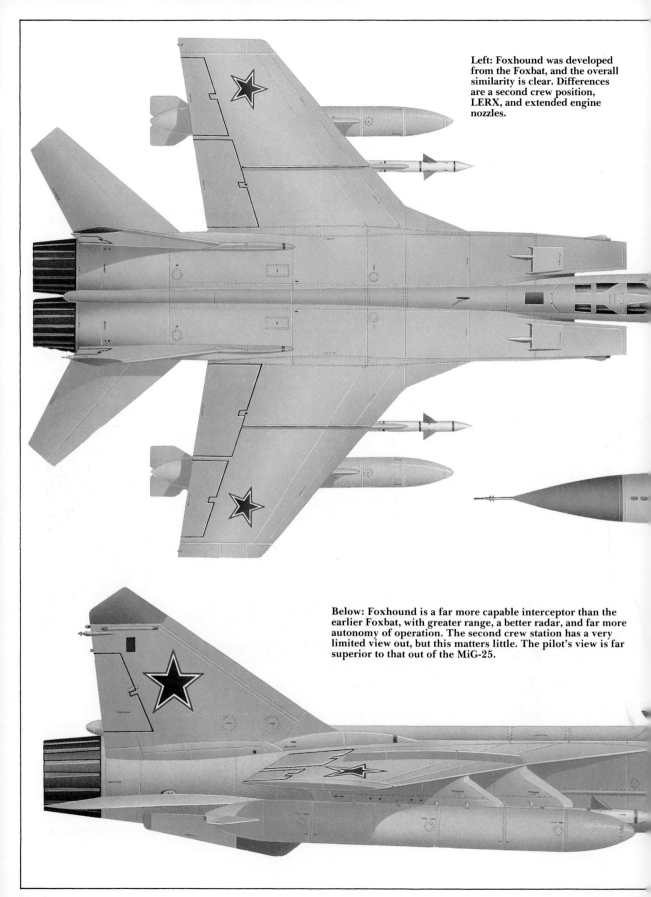

Left: Foxhound was developed from the Foxbat, and the overall similarity is clear. Differences are a second crew position, LERX, and extended engine nozzles.

Below: Foxhound is a far more capable interceptor than the earlier Foxbat, with greater range, a better radar, and far more autonomy of operation. The second crew station has a very limited view out, but this matters little. The pilot's view is far superior to that out of the MiG-25.

Below: The underfuselage carriage of the main missile armament came as a surprise to the West. The missiles are AA-9s and resemble the AIM-54 Phoenix.

Right: Foxhound retains its underwing pylons and can carry two AA-6 Acrid missiles as well as its main AA-9 armament.

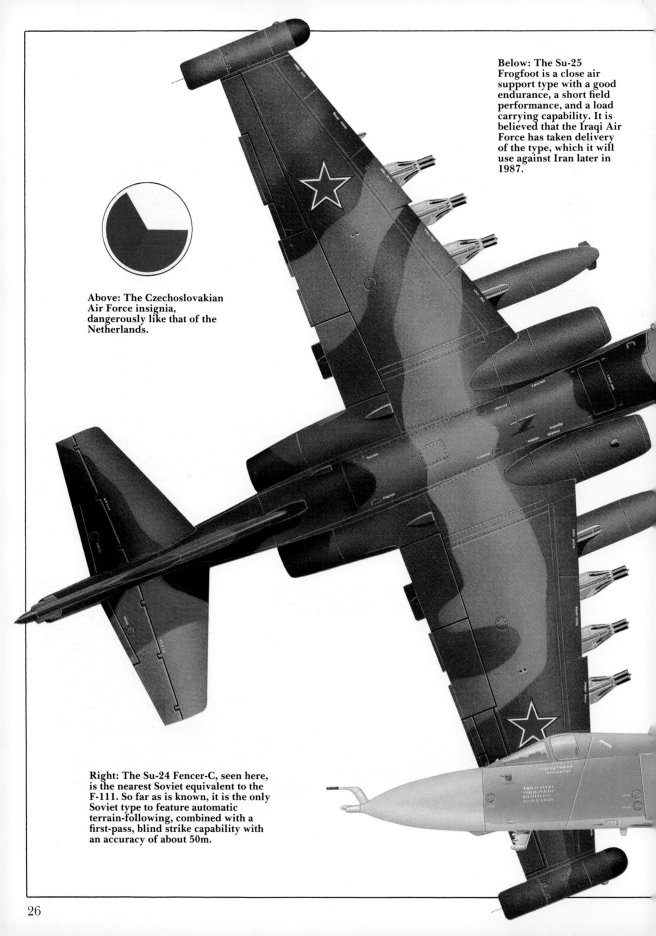

Below: The Su-25 Frogfoot is a close air support type with a good endurance, a short field performance, and a load carrying capability. It is believed that the Iraqi Air Force has taken delivery of the type, which it will use against Iran later in 1987.

Above: The Czechoslovakian Air Force insignia, dangerously like that of the Netherlands.

Right: The Su-24 Fencer-C, seen here, is the nearest Soviet equivalent to the F-111. So far as is known, it is the only Soviet type to feature automatic terrain-following, combined with a first-pass, blind strike capability with an accuracy of about 50m.

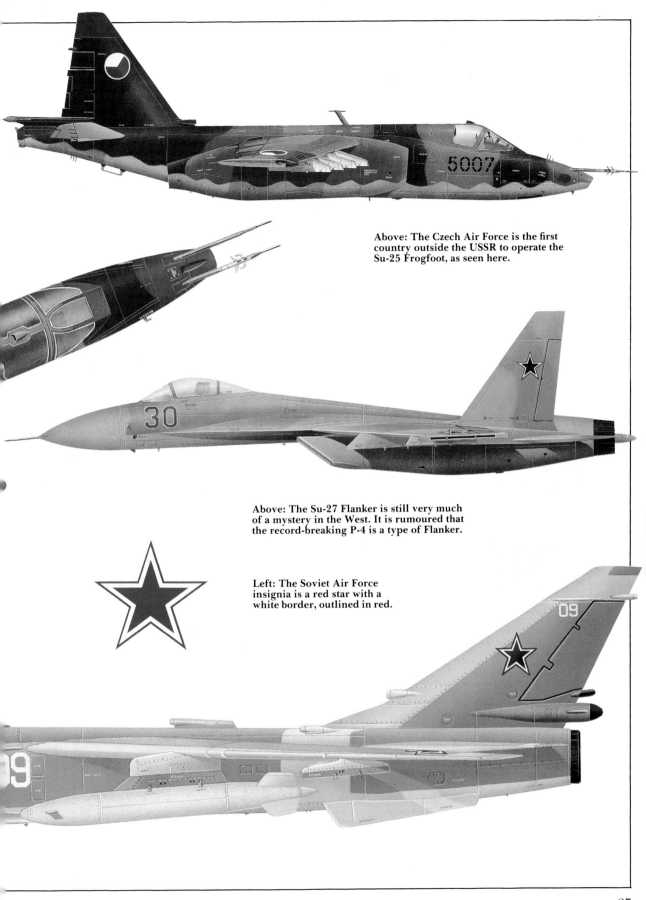

Above: The Czech Air Force is the first country outside the USSR to operate the Su-25 Frogfoot, as seen here.

Above: The Su-27 Flanker is still very much of a mystery in the West. It is rumoured that the record-breaking P-4 is a type of Flanker.

Left: The Soviet Air Force insignia is a red star with a white border, outlined in red.

Below: A Soviet Air Force Frogfoot is seen here with a load of rocket pods and drop tanks. Though camouflaged on top, the underside is light.

Above: So far as is known, the USSR has no equivalent either to the massive GAU-8 tank busting gun or to Maverick, and this must call into question the future of the Su-25 Frogfoot in Soviet service.

Below: Frogfoot's engines are mounted alongside, rather than in the fuselage, which in theory gives plenty of space for fuel. The twin cannon muzzles are set low on the left-hand side of the fuselage.

development aircraft appeared to be positioned on the outside of the engine nacelles, with the "con-di" nozzles projecting behind them, while the very tall, high aspect ratio vertical tails were mounted directly over the engines in a mid-fuselage position. On the production article, the LERXes appear to have been extended past the wing trailing edge to give a "shelf" effect, ending in a stub boom upon which the stabilisers are mounted, while the fins, which have an absolutely straight leading edge, have been moved outboard on to the shelf. It is reasonable to expect that difficulties were encountered in high-AOA flight, either because the fins were blanketed by the forebody, or perhaps because an unfavourable interaction with the vortices shed by the LERX was being produced. Oddly, the seemingly obvious step of canting the fins outboard has not been taken. At the same time, the four very deep wing fences sported by early aircraft were deleted, indicating that the LERX were working properly and rendering them superfluous.

Missile carriage

To date there is no sign of an internal cannon, although there can be little doubt that a gun of some sort is fitted, possibly in one of the LERXes. The normal missile armament is said to be either six AA-10 medium-range radar homers or four AA-10s supplemented by two AA-11 heat-seekers. This does not seem enough: a fighter of this size and power should be able to carry more without undue adverse effects on either performance or handling. The tunnel between the engine nacelles is larger than that of Fulcrum, and does not have the nose gear retracting into it, and so at least two missiles could be carried semi-submerged here, and, as an alternative, missiles could be carried on the undersides of the nacelles, there being sufficient clearance, or conformally along the sides, like the Sparrow carriage adopted by the FAST-equipped F-15C. In addition, there should be either two or three hardpoints beneath each wing. Flanker is also assumed to be able to carry air-to-ground weapons. A load of 13,220lb (6,000kg) has been quoted, made up of twelve 1,100lb (500kg) bombs.

It is to be expected that Flanker is equipped for in-flight refuelling, with a retractable probe located in one of the LERXes. Fulcrum may also have this facility, but the aircraft visiting Finland showed no signs of it.

Service entry

Production of Flanker was initiated at Komsomolsk, in the far east of the Soviet Union, around 1980–81, but hold-ups, variously attributed to airframe revisions, delays in engine delivery or problems with the radar, held back service entry until 1986. Mass production on the lines of, say, Flogger is not anticipated, and a total of just over 600 aircraft are expected to be delivered by 1994.

Flanker is fast and has a good ceiling and a high rate of climb. Calculated figures credit it with a better turn rate than Fulcrum: at Mach 0.9 and 15,000ft (4,570m) the sustained turn is given as 17deg/sec and instantaneous turn as 23deg/sec. Acceleration is supposed to be some 20 per cent faster than that of Flogger, but this is not saying much. If correct, the turn figures are rather better than those of the F-15, but are inferior to those attained by the more modern EFA and Rafale.

A "navalised" Flanker?

It is widely rumoured that a "navalised" Flanker is under development for the new Soviet aircraft carrier of around 65,000 tonnes currently under construction. While it cannot be categorically stated that this is impossible, the difficulties of adapting a very large fighter such as Flanker to shipboard life would seem to be extreme. While it is true that the F-14 Tomcat is heavier, it has the advantage of variable-sweep wings with a battery of high-lift devices to reduce approach speeds to acceptable limits. At one stage a navalised F-15 was proposed, but the problems proved to be difficult if not insuperable, while the "navalisation" of the Northrop YF-17 Cobra into the McDonnell Douglas F/A-18 Hornet involved a considerable increase in both size and weight. For a Navy without orthodox fast jet carrier experience, it seems to be a very tall order.

Flanker has allowed the Soviet Union to catch up with the West rather than surpass it. Fighter development in East and West is currently out of synchronisation, with the West about to step ahead just at the time when the East will have built enough Flankers to pose a serious threat.

4

Mikoyan MiG-25 Foxbat and MiG-31 Foxhound

THE MiG-31 FOXHOUND is so obviously derived from, and shares so many common features with, the MiG-25 Foxbat, that it is difficult to separate the two aircraft without a great deal of repetition, and so they are combined under a single heading. As we saw in the introduction, the development of Foxbat appears to have been initiated as a counter to the B-70 Valkyrie, and continued even after this threat had receded, most probably to give a credible interception capability against the B-58 Hustler, the SR-71 Blackbird, and any fast, high-flying aircraft that the United States might field at some future point. In fact, it had little or no interception capability against the SR-71, but the complete failure of Western intelligence to interpret correctly the true function and capability of the Soviet machine led to the banning of overflights by

Below: Two enormous engines and a huge and powerful radar dominate the design of the MiG-25 Foxbat. This Foxbat-E is the most recent (and probably the final) variant of the type.

MIKOYAN MiG-25 FOXBAT RECORDS

SPEED RECORDS

Date	Pilot	Event	Speed
16 Mar 65	A. Fedotov	1,000km closed-circuit with 1,000kg and 2,000kg payloads	1,252kt (2,320km/h, Mach 2.185)
5 Oct 67	M. Komarov	500km closed-circuit	1,609kt (2,981km/h, Mach 2.808)
27 Oct 67	P. Ostapenko	1,000km closed-circuit with 1,000kg and 2,000kg payloads	1,576kt (2,920km/h, Mach 2.75)
8 Apr 73	A. Fedotov	100km closed-circuit	1,406kt (2,605km/h, Mach 2.45)
2 June 75	S. Savitskaya	Women's absolute speed	1,448kt (2,683km/h, Mach 2.53)
21 Oct 77	S. Savitskaya	Women's 500km closed-circuit	1,331kt (2,466km/h, Mach 2.32)

ALTITUDE RECORDS

Date	Pilot	Event	Height
5 Oct 67	A. Fedotov	Absolute with 1,000kg and 2,000kg payloads	98,355ft (29,977m)
25 July 73	A. Fedotov	Absolute	118,903ft (36,240m)
25 July 73	A. Fedotov	Absolute with 1,000kg and 2,000kg payloads	115,491ft (35,200m)
22 July 77	A. Fedotov	Absolute with 1,000kg and 2,000kg payloads	121,659ft (37,080m)
31 Aug 77	S. Savitskaya	Women's sustained	69,590ft (21,210m)
31 Aug 77	A. Fedotov	Absolute	123,530ft (37,650m)

TIME TO ALTITUDE RECORDS

Date	Pilot	Altitude	Time
4 June 73	B. Orlov	20,000m (65,620ft)	169.8sec
4 June 73	P. Ostapenko	25,000m (82,085ft)	192.6sec
4 June 73	P. Ostapenko	30,000m (98,430ft)	243.86sec
19 May 75	A. Fedotov	25,000m (82,085ft)	154.2sec
19 May 75	P. Ostapenko	30,000m (98,430ft)	189.7sec
19 May 75	A. Fedotov	35,000m (114,835ft)	251.3sec

the Blackbird and the consequent loss of the intelligence data that these could have provided. On the other hand, it is only fair to state that overestimating the capabilities of an opponent is a potentially less lethal error than underestimating them.

Having first flown during 1964, Foxbat came to the attention of the West on 16 March 1965, when a Ye-266 prototype piloted by A. Fedotov broke the world speed record for the 1,000km closed circuit with both 1,000 and 2,000kg payloads, registering a speed of 1,252kt (2,320km/h), or Mach 2.185. Satellite photography and rumour apart, little else was revealed until, more than two years later, on 9 July 1967, four pre-production aircraft were displayed at Domodedovo, when it was announced that they were capable of Mach 3. This demonstration was followed in October of that year by the setting of three further world records (see table), of which the 500 and 1,000km closed circuit speed records had previously been held by the Lockheed YF-12A. These impressive feats set the West agog, and if any commentators stopped to wonder why no attempt had been made on the absolute speed and absolute altitude records, also held at that time by the YF-12A, they probably assumed that this had been precluded by Soviet security considerations.

Over the next ten years, modified Foxbats set no

Above: The absolute speed and 1,000km closed circuit records are now held by the SR-71, and time to altitude records below 20,000m by Streak Eagle (except 3,000m, held by the P-4).

fewer than fifteen further records, including three for time-to-altitude that had previously been held by the F-4B Phantom. Early in 1975 the United States replied with the F-15 Streak Eagle, which made a clean sweep of all the previous time-to-height records, most of which still stand, but on 19 May of the same year Foxbat, in the form of the Ye-266M, recovered the records for 25,000 and 30,000m and set a new time for the 35,000m level. It should, however, be noted that record-breaking is a reflection of national pride rather than operational capability, and is normally carried out by specially modified aircraft. On the other hand, it may reasonably be inferred that while Foxbat's performance is excellent at very high altitudes, it is not so good lower down.

Capabilities overestimated

For many years Foxbat's capabilities were grossly overestimated by the West, and the mythology was compounded by overflights of Sinai by the MiG-25R reconnaissance variant between October 1971 and March 1972, which proved impossible to intercept by the Israeli Phantom/Sparrow combination. Ground radar tracked one of these flights at a speed of Mach 3.2, and it was assumed that this was a normal operational capability, although the aircraft concerned suffered engine damage and barely managed to return to base. It was not appreciated at the time that this was the inevitable consequence of engine overspeeding. Then, in September 1976, Lt. Viktor Belenko defected to the West, landing his Foxbat-A at Hakodate in Japan and allowing a true assessment of the aircraft to be made.

Ram-air effect

The MiG-25 was revealed to be both enormous and genuinely crude, although the aerodynamic design was sound. Power was provided by two huge single-shaft turbojets which were optimised for the top right-hand corner of the envelope at the expense of performance and economy at lower speeds and altitudes. To achieve this, they featured a transonic compressor, which has no Western equivalent, and relied heavily on the ram-air effect at high speeds. The engines are often referred to as turbo-ramjets. To achieve the desired performance, vast amounts of fuel had to be carried—more than 14 tonnes, in fact, giving a fuel fraction of 0.38, which was very high by fighter standards. The gross take-off weight was about five tonnes more than Western analysts had previously calculated, owing mainly to the fact

that the construction was nearly all nickel steel, with little titanium used. Aluminium had been used only in areas of low kinetic heating, such as control surfaces.

Foxbat-A was an optimised point-defence interceptor, with a combat radius of around 400nm (740km) but a flat-out interception radius of only about 160nm (296km). No concessions had been made for close combat: with a full fuel load the limiting g factor was less than 3, while at 50 per cent fuel, a figure that would be reached by the end of the climb and acceleration phase of the intercept, it was still no more than 5. The "red line", never-exceed speed was Mach 2.8, although this could be achieved with a full missile load of four Acrids. The pilot was buried deep in the fuselage, with a poor forward and non-existent rearward visibility. For the mission envisaged, this hardly mattered: most of it could be flown automatically via data link from the ground, leaving the pilot responsible for take-off, radar-acquisition, missile-launch, breakaway and landing, acting as a system manager for the rest of the time with a special responsibility for monitoring fuel state.

The appearance of the MiG-25 is dominated by the engines, which have massive, sharply raked, two-dimensional intakes, with variable ramps, a variable lower lip and outlets for the intake bleed air on the

The Foxbat-A flown in by Lt. Viktor Belenko stands in the over-run area at Hakodate, Japan, September 1976. The great Foxbat myth was finally demolished.

top surfaces, Two huge, fully variable nozzles fill the rear. The Foxfire radar in the nose has a scanner dish some 2.8ft (85cm) in diameter, and this is a factor in sizing the cross-section of the forward fuselage. Foxfire has an estimated power output of 600kW, and was designed to burn through jamming (the Valkyrie bomber was known to carry a state-of-the-art ECM suite). Maximum radar range is quoted as a mere 50nm (90km), but the target RCS to which this applies is not known. Valkyrie is believed to have had an RCS that was an order of magnitude larger than that of the B-52, which is a byword for radar reflectivity. While the technology was of the vacuum tube era, there is little doubt that Foxfire could adequately fulfil its intended mission.

The pilot sits beneath a starboard-hinged canopy with a central spine frame, the rearmost portion of which is metal clad. The canopy tapers, via the avionics compartment, into a dorsal spine housing controls and systems, which terminates in a cone for the double braking parachute. The single-wheel main gear retracts into the sides of the engine intake, while the twin-wheel nose gear is located slightly forward of the bottom lips of the intakes and retracts forwards to stow just behind the cockpit.

The shoulder-mounted wings are of simple planform, with a straight leading edge of 40 degrees sweep; some sources state that the sweep is compound, but this is an optical illusion, caused by a reduction of incidence outboard. Two wing fences

Above: A maintenance crew give scale to the Foxbat, which is huge, and has a pair of the thirstiest engines ever. Note that the wing pylon aligns with the fence on the top surface.

are fitted to each side, the inner one being much the deeper of the two, while tip fairings contain CW radar target illuminators, Sirena III RWR aerials, and static dischargers. Short ailerons are set at mid-span, with flaps inboard on the trailing edge.

Large twin fins

The large twin fins have an almost straight leading edge, with just the slightest increase in sweep where they meet the fuselage, and the raked tips both have dielectric panels housing aerials. A Sirena III RWR projects from the starboard raked tip, while the port leading edge houses an HF aerial. Mounted just outboard of the engines, the fins have a slight outward cant, and a small bulge on each inside surface conceals the actuator for the single-section rudder. Added directional stability is given by twin ventral fins, both of which house aerials and incorporate bumpers at the rear ends to protect the aircraft from the effects of over-rotation. A centrally mounted, ventral air brake is fitted. The horizontal tail surfaces are single-piece, all-moving units, set below the level of the wings. The tips are cropped in the usual Soviet style, presumably as a precaution against flutter.

Weaponry is carried on four underwing pylons,

which align with the wing fences. The missile developed specifically for Foxbat is the very large and heavy AA-6 Acrid, which comes in both semi-active radar-homing (SARH) and infra-red (IR) homing versions. Acrid is carried singly on the pylons, with IR Acrids on the inner pylons and SARH Acrids outboard. These were high-altitude missiles designed to counter Valkyrie, but both AA-7 Apex and AA-8 Aphid have since been carried.

Dedicated reconnaissance version

The Soviet Union is noted for screwing every ounce of capacity from a proven design, and Foxbat has been no exception. The next variant to emerge was the MiG-25R, or Foxbat-B, which entered service in 1971. This features a reconfigured nose, housing both vertical and oblique cameras and sideways-looking airborne radar (SLAR), and is a dedicated reconnaissance aircraft. It has a slightly reduced wingspan, but in other respects appears to be the same as Foxbat-A, although no weapons are carried. It was these aircraft that flew the missions over Sinai in 1971–72, a flight distance of roughly 500nm (927km), and the improved range seems to have been accounted for by the absence of drag-inducing missiles, a reduced afterburner climb, and holding the speed down to about Mach 2.5. The use of drop

Above: A two-seat conversion trainer for the MiG-25 was needed, and the result was the MiG-25U Foxbat-C, with a revised nose containing a second cockpit.

tanks cannot be discounted either, although Foxbat-A was not plumbed to take them and there has been no confirmation that they were used. MiG-25Rs also made numerous flights over Iran, until the Imperial Iranian Air Force carried out live Phoenix missile tests with their new Tomcats in 1976, whereupon the overflights abruptly ceased.

A high-performance fighter almost invariably needs a two-seater conversion trainer to accustom pilots to the type, and the next variant to be identified was the MiG-25U, or Foxbat-C. First seen in 1973, Foxbat-C appears to be a conversion of both A and B types, as individual aircraft appear to differ in detail. A separate cockpit has been added forward and well clear of the original, displacing the radar. The type can therefore have no operational capability, even though the wing pylons have been retained on some aircraft.

Foxbat-D is yet another reconnaissance machine, but dedicated to electronic intelligence (elint) missions. A large SLAR is carried, apparently of two different types (which may indicate two different Foxbat sub-variants), and the shape of the nose has been amended to suit. It retains the reduced wing span of the earlier Foxbat-B, and otherwise has the same configuration except for the nose and a smaller blister for the doppler radar, whilst further flush dielectric panels are visible.

More versatile radar

The final Foxbat type, the E, is another interceptor, and reports are very conflicting. It is stated to have a beefed-up airframe to improve manoeuvre capability, to carry the much more versatile High Lark radar as fitted to the MiG-23 Flogger, combined with a mix of AA-7 and AA-8 missiles, and to have been re-engined with the same powerplant as that selected for the MiG-31 Foxhound. It is not a new-build aircraft, but an updated Foxbat-A. Improved man-oeuvre capability, with higher g limits, would not come amiss. One of two methods could have been adopted—either a total rebuild or merely the addition of a few structural tucks and gussets. The first solution would be difficult, due to the extensive use of welded steel in the structure, while the second can hardly be expected to yield more than a marginal improvement. High Lark radar in place of Foxfire,

together with newer missiles, would make the whole system much more useful, and would be a sensible modification. More powerful and more economical engines would make a great deal of sense, but the use of the same powerplants as those installed in Foxhound does not quite add up, for several reasons. A comparison of the main intakes does not match up, while the nozzles seen on Foxhound are much longer. Finally, Foxbat-E is credited with much the same performance as Foxbat-A, while Foxhound is believed to be limited to a Vmax of Mach 2.4. It is hardly likely that a new engine has been developed specifically for this upgrade, but it is just possible that the original engine has been "tweaked" a little to improve subsonic performance and specific fuel consumption (sfc). The external changes which mark Foxbat-E are a revised radome shape with an IR seeker below, revised antennae on the fins, what appear to be twin blister fairings beneath the cockpit, and different antennae on the

Below: Foxbat-E seen using afterburner. The original MiG-25 was a dedicated, automated interceptor, tied into a rigid ground control system. Foxbat-E is much more flexible.

MIKOYAN MiG-25 FOXBAT/MiG-31 FOXHOUND SPECIFICATION DATA

Dimensions	MiG-25 Foxbat-E	MiG-31 Foxhound-A
Length:	71ft 4in (21.74m)	72ft 6in (22.10m)
Span:	46ft 0in (14.02m)	46ft 0in (14.02m)
Height:	18ft 6in (5.64m)	18ft 6in (5.64m)
Wing area:	662sq ft (61.52sq m)	662sq ft (61.52sq m)
Aspect ratio:	3.27	3.27
Weights		
Empty:	44,000lb (19,960kg)	47,500lb (21,545kg)
Fighter take-off:	82,500lb (37,420kg)	85,000lb (38,556kg)
Maximum take-off:	82,500lb (37,420kg)	90,500lb (41,000kg)
Combat, 50% fuel:	68,710lb (30,260kg)	69,000lb (30,300kg)
Powerplant		
Two Tumanskii	R-31	RD-F
Maximum thrust:	27,120lb (12,305kg)	32,000lb (14,520kg)
Military thrust:	20,500lb (9,301kg)	22,000lb (9,982kg)
Fuel		
Internal:	31,575lb (14,320kg)	32,000lb (14,520kg)
External:	Nil	6,868lb (3,120kg)?
Fraction:	0.38	0.38
Loadings		
Wing, fighter, take-off:	125lb/sq ft (608kg/sq m)	128lb/sq ft (627kg/sq m)
Wing, combat:	101lb/sq ft (492kg/sq m)	104lb/sq ft (509kg/sq m)
Thrust, maximum, fighter, take-off/ combat:	0.66/0.81	0.75/0.93
Thrust, military, fighter, take-off/ combat:	0.50/0.61	0.52/0.64
Performance		
Vmax, hi:	Mach 2.82	Mach 2.4
Vmax, lo:	Mach 0.85	Mach 0.95
Ceiling:	78,000ft (23,800m)	75,000ft (22,900m)
Initial climb rate:	41,000ft/min (208m/sec)	41,000ft/min (208m/sec)
Take-off run:	4,528ft (1,380m)	"Long"
Landing run:	7,152ft (2,180m)	"Long"
Combat radius:	400nm (740km)	800nm (1,480km)
Intercept radius:	160nm (296km)	400nm (740km)

wing-tip pods. The nozzles also appear to be slightly larger in diameter, and to have larger and fewer petals, but this is difficult to judge.

When in 1976 Lieutenant Belenko arrived in Japan, he brought with him the information that the MiG-25 was being developed into a far more capable aircraft designed to counter the Rockwell B-1 bomber. At first thought to be designated the MiG-25MP, this Soviet fighter has since emerged as the MiG-31, and has been allocated the reporting name Foxhound. Little was known about it at first, except that it had a two-man crew, had a look-down, shoot-down capability, entered service in 1982, and looked very much like a Foxbat. Then, in late 1985, a Foxhound was seen and photographed by a Norwegian F-16 off the coast of Northern Norway, and further details became evident.

Foxhound features

Foxhound appears to be a slightly "stretched" Foxbat, with a shorter, more rounded nose cone and extended intakes. The pilot is located further forward than in Foxbat, with rather better visibility than was the case with the earlier aircraft. The weapons systems officer is seated in tandem, beneath what appears to be a metal canopy with transparencies to the sides only. The afterburner nozzles are larger than had previously been represented, and much

Below: The pilot of Foxbat is buried deep in the fuselage of the aircraft, with a restricted view out. The subtle change of section behind the radome is well shown here.

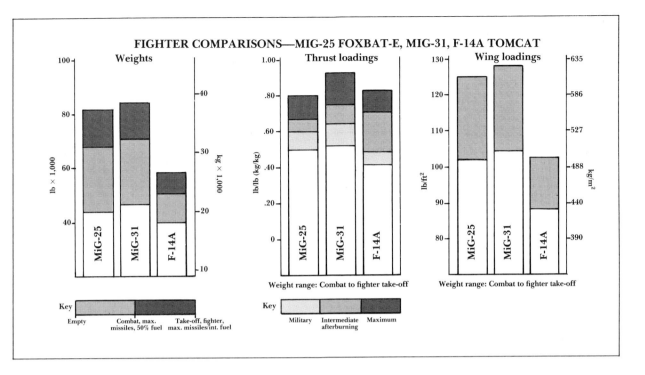

FIGHTER COMPARISONS—MIG-25 FOXBAT-E, MIG-31, F-14A TOMCAT

Weights

lb × 1,000 / kg × 1,000

MiG-25, MiG-31, F-14A

Key: Empty | Combat, max. missiles, 50% fuel | Take-off, fighter, max. missiles/int. fuel

Thrust loadings

lb/lb (kg/kg)

MiG-25, MiG-31, F-14A

Weight range: Combat to fighter take-off

Key: Military | Intermediate afterburning | Maximum

Wing loadings

lb/ft² / kg/m²

MiG-25, MiG-31, F-14A

Weight range: Combat to fighter take-off

---

longer, reaching back past the trailing edge of the horizontal stabilisers. The fins each have a small horizontal surface located just under the dielectric tips on the outside only, and also what appears to be a short root fairing at the base of the leading edge. The bullet fairing mounted dorsally above the nozzles is now raised, and ends as the nozzles begin.

The wings differ considerably in detail. They have sprouted short and apparently sharp-edged LERXes, and the entire trailing edges are given over to control surfaces. These are probably, although

Above: Both Foxbat-E and Foxhound are large and heavy, and apart from top speed and altitude capability are inferior in all departments to the F-14A, the nearest Western equivalent.

not certainly, in three sections, with flaperons on the outer section. The wing tip is squared off, and appears to consist of some kind of fairing, with a rolled end. It can only be assumed that this houses ECM gear. Only one wing fence is to be seen, located

Below: Foxbat had but one purpose, to intercept supersonic bombers at high altitude. For this it carried a quartet of very large missiles, AA-6 Acrids, seen here.

at about one-third of the span, and on the Foxhound photographed only one pylon was visible, directly beneath the fence, which may well indicate that only two wing pylons are now carried as the main missile armament is situated beneath the fuselage. It seems unlikely that there are any moving surfaces to the leading edge of the wing, as the fence extends to the very edge. It is not known whether the wing hardpoints are plumbed for tanks, although this seems possible. As a matter for speculation, all pylons on Foxbat were very deep in order to accommodate the large missiles carried, and those of Foxhound appear also to be very deep, and with the usual Russian gift for making a virtue out of a necessity it may just be that the pylons were designed to give extra keel area to increase the aircraft's lateral stability.

Multi-mode radar

Foxhound is stated to have a powerful multi-mode pulse-doppler radar, based on Western technology, and in particular the Hughes AWG-9, acquired through Iran. This would give it a good look-down capability, while the AA-9 missiles appear to bear a certain similarity of appearance to the AIM-54 Phoenix, which could have been acquired from the same source. As AA-9 was designed specifically for use with Foxhound, a certain similarity of performance cannot be discounted. It has been tested in the look-down, shoot-down mode from as far back as

Above: The MiG-31 Foxhound is a two-seat Foxbat derivative which carries its main armament of four AA-9 missiles under the fuselage while retaining wing pylons.

1978, and has apparently performed well. The underbody missile carriage caught the West completely on the hop, especially one seemingly authoritative commentator who is on record as saying that it was precluded by the main gear position.

Better manoeuvrability

Foxhound is widely rumoured to include a flight refuelling probe, but as yet this has not been confirmed. It certainly has different engines from those of the earlier fighter, and it is equally certain that these are not turbofans. As with Foxbat, we do not know the operational requirement for Foxhound. It is supposed to have Vmax of Mach 2.4, but this is based on the assumption that the Russians have gone for range or endurance rather than Vmax. It is also believed to have better manoeuvre capability and higher g load limits than Foxbat. Certainly, much of the steel construction could have been replaced by titanium, lightening the aircraft considerably, but Department of Defense figures show Foxhound to be heavier. Foxhound is also rumoured to carry an internal gun. If this is the case, the location is yet to be identified; moreover, since the aircraft can hardly be considered a close combat fighter (even if all the rumours are true), there seems little point in having one.

5

Sukhoi Su-24 Fencer

OFTEN DESCRIBED as the most serious Soviet air threat to NATO, the Su-24, reporting name Fencer, is believed to have first flown in prototype form in 1970, entering service six years later. Western intelligence ran true to form, at first misidentifying it as the Su-19, and the tendency to "mirror-image" new Soviet aircraft in the likeness of their Western counterparts was encouraged by certain similarities to the General Dynamics F-111—in fact, Fencer has been described as a "mini-111". This is unfair, as although the Soviet machine is certainly smaller and lighter than the General Dynamics fighter, there is not all that much difference either dimensionally or by weight. The F-111 has a longer range by virtue of its more economical turbofan engines and a much higher fuel fraction, but the Su-24 can carry a rather heavier warload externally. In practice, it is far more probable that the USSR formulated a broadly compara-

ble operational requirement, and many of the answers came out much the same. The suggestion that Fencer is a copy of the Aardvark hardly holds water.

Fencer appears to be the first genuine Soviet aircraft to have an adverse-weather or night deep interdiction and strike capability, with a respectable combat radius in the lo-lo-lo mission, using terrain-following, or possibly terrain-avoidance, to stay below the radar. It has an advanced weapons delivery and nav/attack system with an accuracy stated to be roughly 55m (180ft) in a first-pass, blind strike. Judging by the number of dielectric panels and aerials that have proliferated all over it, Fencer also has a comprehensive internal ECM suite.

Below: The Su-24 Fencer was at first mistakenly identified as the Su-19. This early artist's impression was about par for the course as regards accuracy, as a comparison with the subsequent photographs will show. Initially described as a "mini-F-111", Fencer has little in common other than role.

The main drivers in the design were night and adverse-weather capability, ultra-low-level penetration, extended (by Soviet standards) range, and, in common with the majority of Soviet fast jets, good short field performance. The engines selected were afterburning Lyulka AL-21F turbojets, which gave Fencer a better thrust-to-weight ratio than the F-111, both at clean and maximum take-off weights, thus contributing to good short field performance at full power. Using military power, the difference is even more marked, with far more thrust available for high-speed cruising flight, and better acceleration. In the West, it was assumed for many years that the powerplants were turbofans, probably Tumanskii R-29Bs, although it is now known that the Tumanskii engine is a turbojet and that the Soviet Union had no suitable turbofans available at the right time. The outcome of this misapprehension was inevitably that the radius of action was assumed to be rather longer than was actually the case, and when in the early 1980s the truth became known, it was reported that Fencer was less of a threat than had previously been assumed.

One of the most troublesome problems of the F-111 development period had been that the intakes had been set too far downstream from the nose, giving rise to boundary layer problems and distorted airflow. The Sukhoi OKB avoided this difficulty by adopting side-mounted intakes well ahead of the wing gloves, with a vertical splitter plate mounted next to the fuselage in a manner similar to that of the Phantom. No details are available, but variable internal ramps are certainly used. The inlet location gives a very long duct down to the engine face, which might cause some pressure loss. Blow-in doors are situated on the external faces of the ducts, just beneath the start of the wing gloves.

Side-by-side seating

The fuselage is wide, and of a rounded-off, square section behind the large radome, which carries various sensors at its tip. Remarkably, the cockpit features side-by-side seating for the two-man crew, and it is this that has really caused the "mini-111" description, as it is very unusual in a fast jet: apart from Fencer and the F-111, only the firmly subsonic A-6 Intruder has side-by-side seating. It was used on the F-111 in an attempt to "shoe-horn" the aircraft on to a carrier lift by reducing the overall length, but no such reason applies to Fencer; indeed, although crew co-operation is facilitated by side-by-side seating, there are sound operational reasons for not using it, such as enabling the pilot to have an all-round view to evade an attack by fighters. A straight "steal" from the F-111 hardly seems credible, and the most likely reason for its adoption by the Sukhoi OKB is that an exceptionally large radar antenna, or perhaps a multiple array, demanded a radome far wider than the requirements of a single cockpit, with the result that the design bureau again made a virtue of a necessity and squeezed the double cockpit into the available width. This would have little effect on

Below: One of the best pictures to reach the West so far is of this Fencer-B, carrying two enormous drop tanks on the glove pylons and with two empty shoes on pivoting stations.

SUKHOI Su-24 FENCER SPECIFICATION DATA

Dimensions
Length:	65ft 6in (19.96m)
Span, maximum:	56ft 6in (17.22m)
Span, minimum:	33ft 9in (10.29m)
Height:	18ft 0in (5.49m)
Wing area:	452sq ft (42.0sq m)
Aspect ratio:	7.06/2.52

Weights
Empty:	41,890lb (19,000kg)
Clean take-off:	64,000lb (29,000kg)
Maximum take-off:	87,080lb (39,500kg)
Maximum external load:	24,250lb (11,000kg)
Hardpoints:	8

Powerplant
Two Lyulka AL-21F turbojets each rated at 24,250lb (11,000kg) maximum thrust and 16,975lb (7,700kg) military thrust.

Fuel
Internal:	22,045lb (10,000kg)
External:	18,750lb (8,500kg)
Fraction:	0.34

Loadings
Wing, clean, take-off:	142lb/sq ft (691kg/sq m)
Wing, maximum, take-off:	193lb/sq ft (941kg/sq m)
Thrust, maximum clean/ maximum take-off:	0.76/0.56
Thrust, military, clean/ maximum take-off	0.53/0.39

Performance
Vmax, hi:	Mach 2.18
Vmax, lo:	Mach 1.2
Ceiling:	57,400ft (17,500m)
Initial climb rate:	28,000ft/min (142m/sec)
Take-off run:	N/A
Landing run:	N/A

the frontal area, which by and large was already determined, and would probably save a fair amount of weight, as well as providing extra volume. The canopy appears to be a double transparency opening aft, with a multiple-pane, wrap-around windshield. Rear visibility from the cockpit is poor to non-existent, and the rear edge is faired gradually back towards the rear, forming a spine as far as the fin.

High-lift devices

The variable-sweep wings are pivoted about a position almost identical to that on the considerably smaller Flogger, and rather further outboard than on the F-111. High-lift devices are in evidence, with double-slotted, trailing-edge flaps and leading-edge slats to most of the span. The flaps are in three sections, with only the outboard sections operable at

maximum sweep. Control in the rolling plane is given by differentially operating spoilers, augmented at high speeds by the differentially moving tailerons. The spoilers can be operated in unison to dump lift on landing. The variable sweep has three angles—a minimum of 16 degrees, an intermediate setting of 45 degrees and the fully aft sweep of 68 degrees. Fencer is the first Soviet design to utilise this battery of high-lift devices.

The tailerons are, like those of the F-111, set in the plane of the wings, but, unlike the Aardvark's, they are located well aft, causing a significant gap to open. Of one-piece construction, and with their leading edge matching the wing trailing edge at maximum sweep, they have the typical Soviet cropped tips. The

Below: This angle shows exactly how unlike the F-111 Fencer really is. Close examination reveals many dielectric panels and aerials, which indicate a comprehensive avionics suite.

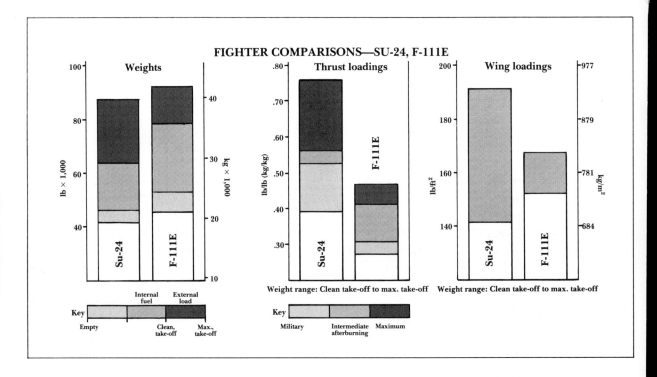

FIGHTER COMPARISONS—SU-24, F-111E

Weights — Thrust loadings — Wing loadings

Above: Often likened to the F-111, this chart shows that the Su-24 is really very different. The smaller fuel fraction and thirsty turbojets of Fencer give it a reduced range.

fin is single, tall and centrally mounted, with a straight leading edge curving into the dorsal spine. The rudder is a single piece of surprisingly large area, and is set just above a large bullet fairing in the trailing edge of the fin. Two small, outward-canted ventral fins assist stability at high speeds and high AOAs.

Underfuselage cannon

Weapons carriage is mainly under the fuselage, on four hardpoints, with a further two beneath the wing gloves. For the first time on a Soviet aircraft, swivelling points were included beneath the movable portions of the wings, to give a total of eight. Contrary to earlier reports of two cannon on the underside of the fuselage, it now seems that there is only one, probably of 23mm calibre and a multi-barrel type, set centrally, far back between the intakes. It has been suggested that this gun is trainable downwards for strafing, and also that it gives Fencer an intruder capability against transport aircraft far out over the Atlantic. These explanations seem a little fanciful. An aircraft as large and expensive as Fencer is hardly going to be used for strafing when there are literally hundreds of much cheaper Floggers available, although of course the cannon might be used as a secondary weapon in an airfield attack involving an

overflight, provided that targets appear under its flight path. In the second case, an air-to-air missile armament would be much preferable, and there is no evidence that this is carried.

The fuel fraction is high for a Soviet aircraft as a result of the range requirement, although not to the extent that it penalises performance as is the case with the F-111. Combat radius has been estimated as 300nm (555km) in the lo-lo-lo mission profile carrying two drop tanks and 4,400lb (2,000kg) of ordnance, increasing to 970nm (1,795km) in the hi-lo-lo-hi profile. It is rumoured that Fencer has, or will have at some point, provision for in-flight refuelling, but this has yet to be confirmed.

To date, three variants have been identified. Fencer-A has a boxed-in appearance beneath the tail pipes, has a rounded fin top, and lacks the large bullet fairing at the fin base; Fencer-B has a contoured underside beneath the tail pipes and a slightly amended rear fuselage; and Fencer-C has a taller fin with a square top, and also varies considerably in the number of excrescences and dielectric panels. The avionics can only be described as comprehensive, with a large forward-looking radar, a TF radar and a doppler, and a laser rangefinder/designator.

6

Sukhoi Su-25 Frogfoot

THE SUKHOI Su-25, reporting name Frogfoot, is a subsonic, single-seat, twin-engined, close air support aircraft. Inevitably it has been likened to the Fairchild A-10, and if ever there was evidence that Western "mirror-imaging" is wishful thinking, Frogfoot is it. The Soviet machine was obviously designed to carry out the same close air support/battlefield air interdiction role but, unlike the Warthog, the Su-25 has not been built around a monster tank-busting cannon, and it has an appreciably higher performance. Nor does it have any similarities in appearance: oddly enough it does resemble a Western type—the Northrop A-9, the Warthog's competitor for the A-X requirement.

First observed at Ramenskoye in 1977 and given the temporary reporting name of Ram-J, Frogfoot entered service about 1981, became operational in Afghanistan in 1982, and has since been exported to Czechoslovakia, Hungary, and Iraq, where it is expected to join action early in 1987. More photographs have been made available in the West than for any other type in this book with the exception of the ageing Foxbat, yet even now little is known for certain. Such basics as dimensions and weights are conflicting and, if analysed, yield figures for wing

Below: The difficulties of an artist having to portray an aircraft from inadequate sources is well illustrated in this early impression of Ram-J, the Su-25 Frogfoot.

SUKHOI SU-25 FROGFOOT CUTAWAY (Schematic)

1. Instrumentation boom.
2. Fire control system transducers.
3. Pitot head.
4. Glazed nose compartment.
5. Laser ranger and marked target seeker.
6. Strike camera.
7. Localiser aerial, port and starboard.
8. Odd Rods IFF antennae.
9. Nose avionics equipment bays.
10. Ventral doppler aerial (starboard side).
11. 23mm six-barrelled rotary cannon (port side).
12. Gun gas venting ducts.
13. Cockpit floor level.
14. Rudder pedals.
15. Front pressure bulkhead.
16. Control column.
17. Instrument panel shroud.
18. Armoured windscreen panels.
19. Pilot's head-up display.
20. Canopy open position.
21. Rear view mirrors.
22. Ejection seat headrest.
23. Pilot's ejection seat.
24. Canopy latch.
25. Seat pan firing handles.
26. Engine throttle levers.
27. Side console panel.
28. Nose undercarriage pivot fixing.
29. Levered-suspension nosewheel forks.
30. Steerable nosewheel (forward-retracting).
31. Mudguard.
32. Nosewheel leg door.
33. Retractable boarding ladder.
34. Fold-out step.
35. Armoured cockpit enclosure.
36. Rear pressure bulkhead.
37. Ejection seat blast screen (retracted).
38. Grab handles.
39. Forward fuselage equipment compartment.
40. Port air intake.
41. Ground power (intercom and telemetry) sockets.
42. Intake ducting.
43. Mainwheel retracted position.
44. Forward fuselage fuel tanks.
45. Wing spar centre section carry-through.
46. Wing panel root attachment bolted joint.
47. Centre section fuel tank.
48. VHF aerial.
49. Starboard wing root attachment joint.
50. Inboard leading edge slat segments (down position).
51. Starboard wing stores pylons.
52. Leading edge dog-tooth.
53. Starboard missile pylon.

54. AA-8 Aphid self-defence air-to-air missile.
55. Outboard leading edge slat segments (down position).
56. Retractable landing/taxying lamp.
57. Dielectric ECM aerial fairing.
58. Starboard navigation light.
59. Wing-tip pod fairing.
60. Split trailing edge airbrakes (open).
61. Static dischargers.
62. Starboard aileron.
63. Aileron tabs.
64. Aileron hydraulic actuator.
65. Starboard double-slotted, Fowler-type flaps (down position).
66. Flap guide rails.
67. Flap jacks.
68. Engine bay venting air intake.
69. Starboard engine installation.
70. Dorsal access panels (controls and systems ducting).
71. Rear fuselage fuel tanks.
72. Fuel systems venting air intake.
73. Enviromental system ram air intake.
74. Tailfin.
75. Starboard trimming tailplane.
76. Starboard elevator.
77. Fin-tip UHF aerial fairing.
78. Tail navigation and position lights.
79. Upper rudder segment.
80. Rudder tabs.
81. Lower rudder segment.
82. Rudder hydraulic actuator.
83. Sirena-3 radar warning antennae.
84. Brake parachute housing.
85. Ventral chaff/flare dispenser.
86. Elevator tab.
87. Port elevator.
88. Static dicharger.

89. Port trimming tailplane.
90. Tailplane pivot fixing.
91. Tailplane incidence control jack.
92. Ventral Odd Rods IFF antennae.
93. Rear fuselage communications and ECM equipment.
94. Ventral Towel Rail HF aerial.
95. Environmental control system equipment.
96. Engine exhaust nozzle.
97. Tumanskii R-13-300 non-afterburning turbojet.
98. Engine bay venting air intake.
99. Accessory equipment gearbox.
100. Flap guide rails.

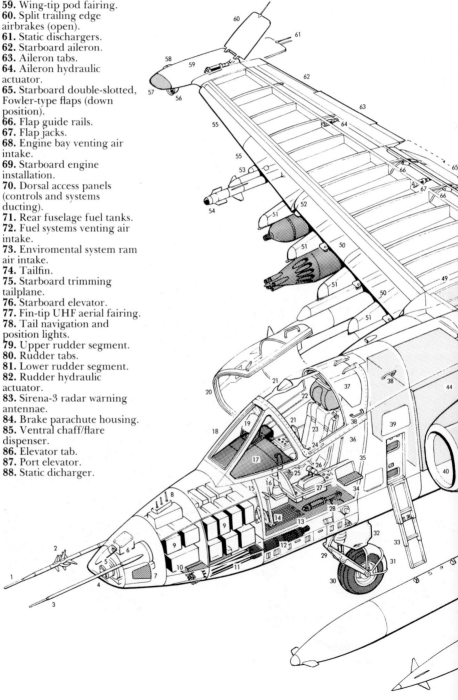

101. Flap control jacks.
102. Two-segment, double-slotted Fowler-type flaps.
103. Aileron tabs.
104. Aileron hydraulic actuator.
105. Port aileron.
106. Split trailing edge airbrake (open).
107. Static dischargers.
108. Airbrake hydraulic jack.
109. Port navigation light.
110. Retractable landing/taxying lamp.
111. Dielectric ECM aerial fairing.
112. Leading-edge slat segments.
113. AA-8 Aphid self-defence air-to-air missile.
114. Missile launch rail.
115. Outboard missile pylon.

116. PAB-500 1,102lb (500kg) HE bomb.
117. UV-16-57 rocket pack (16 × 57mm rockets).
118. 57mm high-velocity aircraft rocket (HVAR).
119. Leading-edge dog-tooth.
120. Port wing stores pylons.

121. Wing rib construction (dry bay, no fuel in wings).
122. Inboard leading-edge slat segments.

123. Port mainwheel.
124. Levered-suspension axle beam.
125. Shock absorber strut.
126. Main undercarriage leg pivot fixing.
127. Hydraulic retraction jack.
128. Leg rotating jack.
129. Mainwheel doors.
130. 132 Imp. gal. (600l) external fuel tank.
131. AS-7 Kerry air-to-surface missile.
132. BETA B-250 551lb (250kg) retarded bomb.

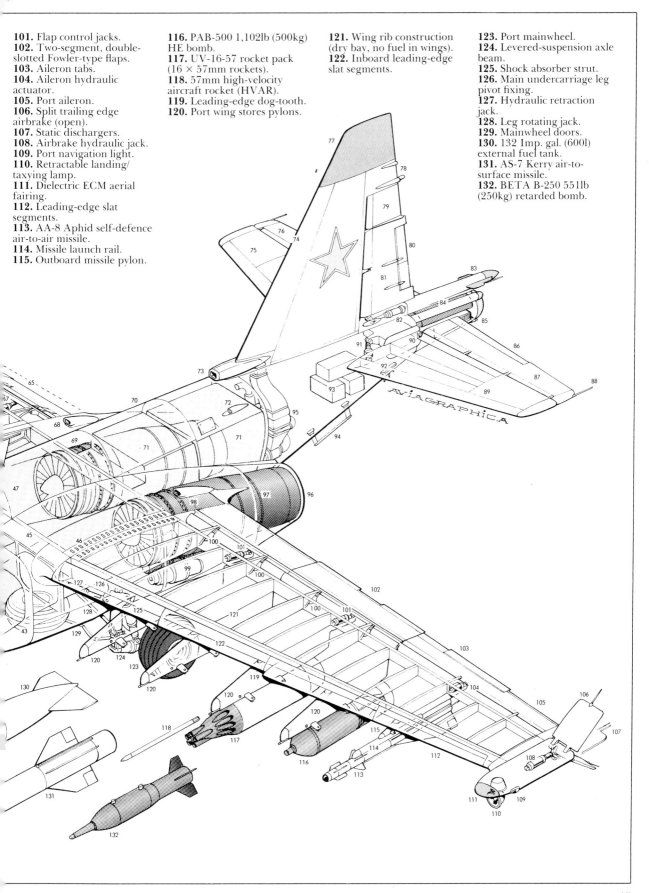

and thrust loading which seem peculiar to say the least. The accompanying data table is an attempt, based on what appears to be the most reliable information for dimensions, to reconcile the discrepancies that the wing loading at maximum take-off weight is rather less than that of the A-10 and that the fuel fraction is 0.30. This leaves the empty weight looking rather high, but the other figures are reasonable. The figures could possibly be accounted for if the Russians have, like the Americans with the A-10, gone for survivability in a big way but using steel instead of titanium, for both armour and some of the structure. While titanium technology in the Soviet Union has come a long way in the past decade, to the point where the country is the largest pro-

Above: Frogfoot is believed to be a counterpart of the A-10A Warthog, but this analogy should not be pursued too closely, as the two differ in many important respects.

ducer in the world, steel remains rather stronger, although heavier, and is much easier to work and very much cheaper. If the Sukhoi OKB could get both the required strength and performance by using steel, considerable savings could be made, so the extensive use of steel remains a possibility. If this conjecture is wrong, and Frogfoot is rather lighter than has been calculated, then the fuel fraction will be higher and the capacity less, while the turbojets

Below: Frogfoot is lighter, has a smaller fuel fraction, and carries a smaller warload than the A-10A, but has a similar wing loading and a vastly superior thrust loading.

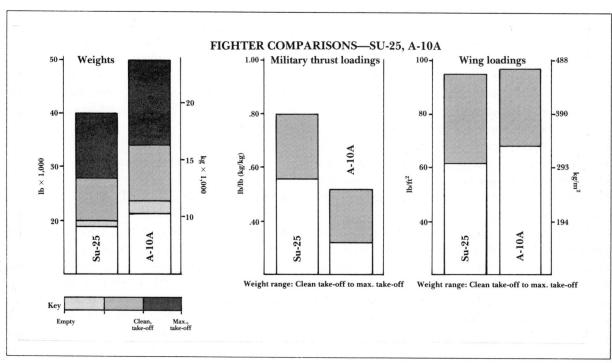

SUKHOI Su-25 FROGFOOT SPECIFICATION DATA

Dimensions

Length:	49ft 2.6in (15.00m)
Span:	46ft 10.8in (14.30m)
Height:	16ft 4.9in (5.00m)
Wing area:	420sq ft (39.00sq m)
Aspect ratio:	5.24

Weights

Empty:	19,200lb (8,709kg)
Clean take-off:	28,000lb (12,700kg)
Maximum take-off:	40,000lb (18,144kg)
Maximum external load:	12,000lb (5,443kg)
Hardpoints:	10

Powerplant

Two Tumanskii R-13-300 turbojets each rated at 11,250lb (5,100kg) military thrust.

Fuel

Internal:	8,400lb (3,810kg)
External:	2,060lb (934kg)
Fraction:	0.30

Loadings

Wing, clean, take-off:	67lb/sq ft (327kg/sq m)
Wing, maximum, take-off:	95lb/sq ft (465kg/sq m)
Thrust, clean/maximum take-off:	0.80/0.56

Performance

Vmax:	Mach 0.74
Ceiling:	N/A
Initial climb rate:	N/A
Take-off run:	1,500ft (457m)
Landing run:	1,200ft (366m)
Operational radius:	300nm (556km)

will appear to be rather oversized and too thirsty for the endurance that Frogfoot has demonstrated over Afghanistan.

Frogfoot's layout is basic, with a squarish fuselage section and two Tumanskii R-13-300 unreheated turbojets mounted in a mid position on each side, apparently angled downwards slightly, which would assist take-off performance. The intakes are plain, rounded at top and bottom, and flattened at the sides, the inner intake face being set slightly away from the fuselage, with no apparent splitter plates. The nose has the semi-chisel shape associated with a laser ranger and possibly a target marker, with a strange recess on the upper surface which is thought to be a cutaway for a strike camera. Two pitot heads project on each side of the recess, that on the right being for instrumentation in connection with the fire control system. The windshield is in three pieces, an optically flat, presumably bulletproof screen flanked by two curved side panels, with the usual heavy framing on which are fixed two rear-view mirrors. The canopy is hinged to open to starboard, and has two transparencies with a central frame, into which latter is let a periscopic central rear-view mirror. The rear portion of the canopy is clad with metal, giving absolutely no rear view beyond that obtainable with the mirrors. The pilot sits fairly high, and his view forward and over the side should be good. The rear of the cockpit fairs straight into the fuselage, with no suggestion of a spine, running through to the end cone, where a Sirena RWR housing, a braking parachute bullet and a chaff/flare dispenser combine to give an untidy effect. The underside of the fuselage remains roughly parallel with the top to a point approximately level with the wing trailing edge, from where it breaks upwards into a taper. A dorsal blade VHF aerial, a ventral Towel Rail HF aerial, and Odd Rods IFF antennae on top of the nose and beneath the tail are the other protrusions seen to date.

Some three-views show a square protrusion on the cockpit sides which has been interpreted as being some form of appliqué armour. The most recent photographs of Frogfoot show no sign of this, and it seems unlikely that it ever existed, as there is a folding step on the left side of the cockpit on to which an access ladder can be hooked, right where this mysterious panel would have been. This step is supplemented by a grab handle located just behind the canopy, and it is believed that folding integral steps might be featured just ahead of the intake on this side.

The gear is short, chunky and obviously designed for rough-field operations. The single-wheel nose gear retracts up under the cockpit floor, and has a light mudguard, while the single-wheel main gears retract into bays beneath the engine ducts. Ground clearance is too little for underfuselage store stations to be used.

Wing design

The wing is shoulder-mounted, of high aspect ratio and thick section, with a leading edge sweep of about 20 degrees, a straight trailing edge and gentle anhedral. The leading edges are taken up with four-piece slats, with what seems to be a dogtooth at mid-span, although why this should be necessary is unclear—the sweep seems too little to warrant it. Pre-production aircraft are believed to have carried wing fences; again, these would hardly appear to be necessary. The trailing edges have ailerons outboard, with just a hint of what look to be tabs, and two-section, double-slotted, Fowler-type flaps inboard. The wing tips carry a strange flattened pod with an ECM housing at the front, beneath which is a retractable landing light, while the rear forms a split airbrake which, it is believed, can operate differentially to assist roll control. The system must be very reliable, as it would be very embarrassing if it malfunctioned on finals. The fin is tall, has a moderate leading edge sweep, and features a ram air intake at the base. It is capped with a large dielectric aerial. The rudder is in two parts, the upper of which is probably a yaw damper. The horizontal tail is unusual in being of two-piece construction with an elevator.

Worthwhile warload

All weapons are carried on underwing hardpoints, eight large with two smaller ones outboard; the purpose of the latter is uncertain, but they are possibly for air-to-air missiles or extra countermeasures pods. The two inboard hardpoints on each side are plumbed for drop tanks. A cannon, probably a 23mm or 30mm multi-barrel type, is carried under the cockpit floor and offset to port. There is no evidence that it is in any way comparable to the gigantic GAU-8/A of the Warthog.

Frogfoot would appear to be a close air support and counter-insurgency aircraft which is easy to fly. Rumour has it that a two-seat version is under development, although conversion training would hardly warrant this; if it does appear it will almost certainly be a night/adverse-weather variant with more sophisticated avionics. The aircraft is heavily protected, has a long loiter time and carries a worthwhile warload, consisting in the main of cluster bomb units (CBU), laser-guided bombs (LGB) and air-to-ground missiles, plus unguided rocket packs.

The Su-25 seems to have taken a long time to enter service, and this has been the cause of considerable speculation, as it is a simple design and the gestation period should have been quite rapid. Its use in Afghanistan suggests that it is effective in the counter-insurgency role, and it is just possible that it was intended mainly for the export market, aimed at Third World countries with internal problems and without the facilities to maintain really sophisticated fighters. If this be the case, it has been a failure, as however effective it may be in its designed role it lacks the cachet of a supersonic fighter and therefore would be less attractive politically.

If used in the close air support role against a modern air defence system, it may or may not prove to be as survivable as the A-10. Certainly, its extra speed would help, at the expense of accuracy of weapons delivery, but it is unlikely that it can absorb as much punishment as the American aircraft, and it is almost certainly nowhere near as reparable.

Below: A nose laser ranger and marked target seeker can be seen, as can the offset cannon muzzle. The folding step just below the cockpit rules out appliqué armour in this area.